GOD MOMENTS GUIDE MY JOURNEY

By

Margie A. Olson

Bee ~
May you see ~
many God Moments
Margie

Dedicated to my children Christine, Paul, and Jane

To my grandchildren Daniel, Lucas, Laura, Joel, Lisa, Carl, Bin Bin, and Ingrid

Copyright © 2018 Margie A. Olson
ISBN: 9781791536350

TABLE OF CONTENTS

INTRODUCTION

I write this book in response to a sense of call in this Bible passage:

"God, you have taught me since I was young,

To this day I tell about the miracles you do.

Even though I'm old and grey, do not leave me God.

I will tell the children about your power;

I will tell those who live after me about your might.

God your justice reaches the skies.

You have done great things (for me)

God there is no one like you." Psalm 71:17-19 New Contemporary Version

My life has changed so much. I made a note in my journal a few weeks after starting internship (1994). "Something startled me this afternoon. I was out at Bethesda Care Center. I had on my red sundress with a white shirt under it. As I entered the door there was this beautiful lady smiling at me. I thought it was someone behind a counter or something and suddenly I realized that beautiful lady was me (in a mirror). It was hard to take it in--hard to believe it was me! I had struggled with self-esteem and this was a me I didn't recognize. Lord, I praise you!"

As I read this today, it still amazes me. I'm the same person who was in a group picture when I was in eighth grade (1944). I looked so sad. I was ashamed of my looks--I couldn't stand to look at it. I scratched off my face. And now with a smile on my face and looking attractive, I couldn't recognize myself! I attribute that to God's pursuing me, drawing me close in grace, in God-Moments where God has revealed his Godself to me.

On these pages I tell my story of how this evolved. Strength to go through incest therapy. (Oh yes, it takes strength to rout up all those buried memories.) Called to seminary when I was sixty years old! Studying while continuing to heal there. Being a pastor, trying to meet parishioners and senior pastor's expectations! God has guided me with God Moments.

STARTING A NEW LIFE

SECTION I

A LUNCH THAT CHANGED MY WORLD

My friend, Verna had recently returned from Papua New Guinea where she had spent two years with her family. She and I had worked together in Grand Rapids at the intensive care unit and later in Public Health department. We arranged a lunch meeting, so I could hear about her latest adventure.

At this meeting, much to my surprise, we spent most of the time talking about that I, too, could have an experience of my own. At the end of the lunch, it amazed me that I had decided to take a sabbatical year from work and explore my dreams. It might be teaching English in Japan or something entirely else.

My husband, Ralph, and I had talked of doing something like this — maybe he would join me. Verna recommended that I go by myself if he wasn't interested. She said, "Everything you do that's important, you do by yourself." I had to think about that. Influenced by my daughter, Chris, I had been doing a daily Bible study. This was strengthening my relationship with God. I would pray about it and see what happened.

I didn't wait long. I was excited! That night I talked to Ralph. No, he didn't want to go anywhere. That wasn't anything he was interested in. He was happy here where we were. But I wanted to do something or go somewhere. So, he guessed if I wanted, I could do this, he said very seriously.

Ralph wouldn't stop me! I was excited. The more I prayed and thought about it, the more interesting it seemed. That weekend I wrote a request for a year's sabbatical leave beginning September first.

Then my exploring started. I talked to my pastor and asked if there was something in the church. I had heard about Lutheran World Hunger taking trips. I would offer six months service. I investigated every reference or advertisement I encountered. I had contact with the possibility of doing nursing in remote Alaska, flying from village to village. Another offer was to work on an Indian reservation in Arizona. A Catholic agency was opening a hospital in Guam that needed a nurse trainer, but that project was delayed time and again. I contacted the ship HOPE, which toured the world bringing medical and surgical help to people. Then the pastor called me one day at work. He was so excited. He had found that our church had a volunteer program, Lutheran World Ministries Volunteers (LWMV), but the director was out of the country, in Nepal, at the time. I wanted to contact the director when he returned, but the pastor said, "No," he'd like to do this for me. When the pastor talked to him several weeks later, amidst other information, he asked if there was financial compensation. The director said, "No, but that's not a problem, is it? She's a member of your congregation," my pastor told me.

There was an application with collected references to be sent to the director who would forward it to those who might be able to use my help. They, in turn, would invite me to join them in their specific ministry. When the director received the application, he called to tell me he was sending it to Liberia and Papua New Guinea. I asked, "Liberia, that's in Africa, isn't it?" "Yes, it is," he replied. "Is that a problem?" "I guess not." I said. I didn't even know where Liberia was.

In the meantime, a request came to go to Cambodia to work with refugees. The time-line was rushed. I was told the support network was weak in this difficult work situation, so after due consideration and prayer, I declined.

I began my sabbatical without an assignment, so I accepted my brother-in-law's offer to help us reface our kitchen cabinets with walnut veneer. It was a project that kept me busy for the next six weeks.

In the first part of November, I was getting restless. I thought about my conversation with Verna about teaching English in Japan, so I called the Chicago immigration office, asking about a Visa to Japan. My Bible reading the next day was from Numbers 22, the story of Balaam on his donkey, being stopped by an angel. It was like I was hearing "Stop!" I was so confused. I had never had an experience like this. I couldn't figure out what was going on. I told my pastor about it and he looked at me puzzled. Three days I prayed and pondered. On the fourth morning, I heard as I read in my God Calling devotional, "You've given it to God, now let God work it out." I said, "OK, God, I'll give you two weeks!"

Two weeks later I received a phone call from the director of LWMV. He said he had a call from Herb Munson whose son, Dr. Mark Munson was in Liberia. Herb had talked to Mark by short wave radio the night before. Dr. Munson asked his father to get a message to me right away that they were going to invite me to Liberia. Their invitation would be delayed because of a government coup attempt, causing an emergency situation. Please call her right away he had said and let her know it will come as soon as possible. At the time I didn't connect the two-week time constraint. Maybe it was because I was confused by the urgency of this strange call. Reflecting later, I am amazed that my timetable was important to God.

How many God moments? The conversation with Verna, the reluctant approval from Ralph, the message and explanation of stop, and God's adhering to my timetable of two weeks. And maybe more.

A CHRISTMAS GIFT

The invitation to fill a teaching position in Zor Zor, Liberia, at the Esther Bacon School of Nursing arrived the day after Thanksgiving. Another invitation came from Papua New Guinea to be a bush nurse working with people the director didn't know — but Verna did. Verna said they were very responsible people. The director said he usually didn't make recommendations, but he did to me. He thought I should go to Liberia and I accepted his advice.

During the months of exploration, I was introduced to a doctor who had done a number of short-term missions. I was eager to talk to him about his experiences. He asked if my husband was also going. When I told him of Ralph's disinterest, his major concern was talking to Ralph. A meeting was arranged. He strongly encouraged Ralph to go with me on this adventure. The doctor told him it would change me, and that change could affect our marriage. Ralph's mind was made up. He was not interested.

I had talked to my daughters and son about Christmas as funds were limited for gift purchases. Chris asked that I sew a blouse and dress for her. The patterns and fabric arrived the same day as the invitation from Liberia. The invitation said, "It would be well if Mrs. Olson could come as soon as possible to get oriented before classes begin after January first."

I looked at the fabric — beautiful rose satin (slippery) for the dress, lovely white, silky fabric for the blouse. Both patterns with pleats and tucks (not simple sewing). "How am I to do this, dear God?" I asked. I'll do what I can.

There were immunization shots, some in Duluth. I was given contact information for a woman who had been teaching at Esther Bacon School. She gave me a vision of the situation there and a lot of information on

5

Africa, on Liberia and on teaching at Zor Zor. There was planning, packing — and sewing.

I had a discussion with my pastor about finances. It was agreed that I would pay for transportation and that congregation groups and individuals would be asked to donate ten dollars a day for maintenance. I was so thankful for this offer of assistance.

I was ready to go in two weeks, except the sewing. The plane I was to take left Amsterdam every Thursday for Monrovia, Liberia. For the first Thursday, I heard on Wednesday afternoon that the Liberian ambassador was tied up in meetings in Washington, D.C. and couldn't sign my visa. The next Wednesday afternoon I was told that because of the beginning of the holiday traffic, there were no seats available on the plane. They secured a ticket for me on Christmas Day. My pastor said, "Christmas Day! You can't go on Christmas Day!" Of course, I could go on Christmas Day. I was a nurse, and I was accustomed to odd things happening on holidays, including Christmas Day. And by then the sewing was completed!

My daughter, Jane, had returned from college for the holidays. She, Ralph and I left Grand Rapids on Christmas Eve Day with the thermometer at -20 degrees. A group from church surprised us, caroling to us from the front lawn and sending me us on my way with song and prayers. How lovely! Chris came from Omaha and my son, Paul, from Chicago to join us in Minneapolis. I brought Christmas Eve dinner which we ate in the motel for our family Christmas celebration. We found a Lutheran congregation nearby to join in celebrating Christ's birth that evening. The next morning, we swam in the pool and at noon I was off to New York City on the first leg of my journey to Zor Zor, Liberia. The family went to western Minnesota to Grandma's to join the extended family celebration.

The director of LWMV met my plane in New York City, shuttling me from one airport to the other, giving me a torn bag of Christmas greetings for the missionaries in Zor Zor and a new wringer for the washing machine which they used for the operating room laundry in the hospital. Most important he gave me a 10 to 15 minute missionary orientation with two memorable suggestions. First, don't expect a red-carpet reception. People have their own lives and sometimes your coming isn't convenient. Second, you think you are doing a great thing by coming, and you are. But, see what you can learn from them. It's a two-way learning situation. And I was off with prayer, an extra suitcase that he convinced the agent to check at no additional charge and an extra bag to carry.

How many God Moments? Arrival of invitation and fabric in same mail delivery; the doctor coming to talk to my husband; the director previously preparing the pastor to financially support me; my delayed departure — sewing completed; scattered family gathering in Minneapolis; meeting, and orientation by my volunteer director on Christmas day. Where have you seen God work in your life?

WHAT AM I DOING HERE IN LIBERIA?

When I arrived in Liberia on Friday, the day after Christmas I was met by Betty, one of our missionaries who had spent her whole adult life working there. She was planning a wedding on Sunday for one of her adopted Liberian daughters. Needless to say, she was not thrilled to have to pick me up at the airport, forty miles from Monrovia where we were both headed that day. I was thankful for my orientation not to expect a red carpet when I arrived. I was certainly inconveniencing Betty, the only one available with a car who could pick me up that day. She was gracious, took me to the church house (located on the beach) where missionaries stayed when in the city. Here I met Ginny, in the city for the holiday, also from Zor Zor, where I would be working. She would become a trusted friend.

Sunny and eighty degrees or more every day! It was minus twenty when I left Grand Rapids. But it's amazing how our bodies adapt! I got to Zor Zor on the "money bus," a minivan that stood in marketplace at 6:30 each morning until it got a load. Since I was white, I was privileged to sit in the middle front seat between the driver and an honored chief. Both of them smoked and they spoke only the Loma language. Behind the partition to the back were crunched in about ten people. Baskets, luggage, mats, and other non-perishables were on the rack on top. Any fruit or vegetable sacks, chickens, etc. were under the benches. It was a long five-hour ride.

I was delivered to Curran Hospital where Dr. Munson met me with warm welcome. He showed me to my apartment in the Esther Bacon House and invited me to dinner. I had been delayed in Monrovia for three days and Grace, his wife had prepared a welcome meal three times! How gracious they were, welcoming me and throughout my stay!

I had a roomy simply furnished apartment (one half of a house) with a kitchen, living room with a sleeping alcove, and bathroom with running cold water. There was an electric refrigerator and two burner hot plate. It was very adequate for me. My invitation was to teach in the Esther Bacon School of Nursing (EBSN).

Esther Bacon was a highly revered nurse missionary who arrived in the early 1940's as the doctors were leaving to serve in WW2. She worked closely with the pregnant women, traveling by horseback, delivering many babies at home. Over the years she was successful in convincing the women to come to the hospital for safe delivery of their babies. She died among them of Lassa Fever in 1973.

I spent those early weeks getting to know the other missionaries, observing in the hospital, meeting the students, and acquainting myself with teaching materials. There were no textbooks for the students, but a Peace Corps volunteer had outlined a medical-surgical textbook. Duplicated copies of this outline would be used by the students.

The mission compound included a bush hospital with about eighty beds. There was an adult, pediatric and maternity wing, with surgery rooms and delivery rooms. Each patient needed an accompanying caregiver who provided clean bed linens, food, toileting and personal care. Nursing provided the medications and the treatments that were ordered, as well as teaching health and nutrition.

On the hospital grounds were cooking stations for relatives of patients, residences for the doctors, and other staff. The missionary group at this time consisted of: Dr. Mark Munson and family; Dick Bjork and his wife, the Hospital Administrator; Ginny, medical technician; and myself, all from USA. The two Doctors Alexander from India were also on the staff as well the director of the nursing school, Mr. Woloba, and the director of the outreach clinic program.

The faculty met in January to discuss the school term. The director felt it would be good to have a review of anatomy and physiology because the class struggled with that last year. Dr. Munson said he would teach that. There would be a class on public health which the director of the clinic program said he would teach later in the year. Other subjects were introduced, and assignments received. Medical-Surgical Nursing was introduced, and everyone looked at me. I said I'd be happy to teach that class.

That, to me, was such a unique gift. No one told me I was to teach Med-surg nursing. It was not in the invitation. Even though in phone conversation while in Minnesota to the lady who had taught at EBSN, I was led to believe that that's what I would do and that's what I had traveled all these miles to do. When the time came, I was asked, silently, to volunteer. I had a choice. To me it was empowering.

We began classes with one hour of Medical-Surgical Nursing five days a week. I had the outline of a Medical-Surgical textbook done by a previous volunteer duplicated, system by system, for each student. Our class consisted of seventeen students. Eight women were nurse-midwifery students and the nine men were practical nursing students.

One night after I was there about two months, I realized I had read almost every book in the small library. True stories about this country — a white woman travelling in the bush, carried on a pallet by four Africans. They had to chop through the bush with their machetes to make a path, communicating along the way village to village with drumming. There were several books by Dr. Dibble, who arrived about this time, written about his experiences in Tanzania. Dr. Dibble, a surgeon, came to teach

10

the doctors more about surgical procedures. I guess loneliness was creeping in and I began to wonder how I could spend another four months here. I went to bed sad that night.

The next morning at 7:30 there was a knock on the door. It was Mrs. Bjork. Would I like to go to Monrovia? There were missionaries from up-country going through, they'd come last night, and I could ride with them. It was the chance for a break that I needed. God planned it for me, knowing what I needed before I did! Someone took my class for the day and I was off for the city with time to reflect and get new perspective.

When I returned on the money bus on Sunday, I was revived and ready to go again. We increased the class to two hours each day which gave me more to do and I started some sewing projects. I was so thankful that God was taking care of me.

Have you experienced that care?

MIRACLE HEALINGS

I came from hospitals that had operating rooms with shiny white walls and floors. They use throw-away syringes and needles. Oh — I knew another way. Washing the syringes and wrapping them. Sharpening the needles on a flint and sterilizing them in the autoclave. We did that when I was in nurses' training 20 years before. And here in Curran Hospital — this bush hospital, it was still done that way. The operating room was clean, and the surgical area is sterile but there was a different atmosphere. Yet God's healing power was apparent to me and those around in miraculous ways.

A man came in one evening who had shrapnel wound in the abdomen. In surgery gunshot was removed as much as possible, damage to intestines and organs repaired, sulfa powder sprinkled in the abdomen and the wound closed. Electric gastric suction was used, but the electricity was turned off twice a day for a total of twelve hours to conserve gasoline consumption by the generator. He recovered without peritonitis! I had seen many cases of peritonitis with less invasive injuries. It seemed like a miracle to me!

Kulo, the ten-year-old son of one of the hospital maintenance workers was admitted with a big open ulcer on the inside of his left wrist extending to his elbow. They removed about two cups of pus. When it was debrided and cleaned the ulnar nerve and tendons were exposed at the wrist. Two to three weeks before he had fallen and injured his arm. He was taken to the local medicine man for treatment with "country medicine." Among other treatments hot leaves that were applied, causing a burn. Dr. Dibble was called to assess the situation. Amputation of the arm was a real possibility, but he wanted to prevent that. He decided to grow a tubular graft of flesh on the boy's abdomen, which would gradually be transferred to the boy's arm to cover the wound. I don't remember how the wound, nerves and tendons were protected. But I do remember seeing those happy parents with their beaming boy displaying his healed wound with a functioning hand. I believe there was limitation of the thumb, but it was there. There was celebration on the mission compound with praise to God and to the surgeon. Many times, the hospital and western medicine were a last resort for the Liberians. Their culture taught that evil spirits caused illness and disease and the medicine man was in charge of warding off evil spirits.

The third example of what seemed like a miracle to me was my experience on a trip to Northwest Liberia. I was blessed to travel with Ginny, our Curran Hospital Lab Technologist and my missionary friend, who had connections with other health clinic labs around the country. So, when she invited me to travel with her for seven days, I went.

We started on Sunday afternoon north to Voinjama by money bus — eighty miles, three hours. Then on to Kohlahun in a pickup with seats in the back, another three hours. There we were met by our host, Pastor Mason, who took us to Vahun where he lived and worked. We travelled through beautiful country, sometimes on a dirt trail, even across a bridge that was only logs over a stream, forty miles in three hours. If someone was in the yard the pastor knew, he'd greet them. We carried medicine for someone, picked up a rider for a short distance, etc. It was like a money-bus but no pay and considerably friendlier.

The purpose of Ginny's trip was to visit various clinics including Vahun clinic and make recommendations for their labs. The Masons had been there for a year and a half. His wife and eldest son had returned to the US, he for college, she for medical care. His daughter, aged 14, entertained ten people for lunch! She rolled out a big stack of tortillas, with a little help (rolling tortillas was a first-time experience for me) and kettle of

13

refried beans! Imagine a fourteen-year -old girl with Liberian contemporaries getting married or having babies. Her only companions were her sixteen-year-old brother and ten-year-old sister. We had a fun hymn sing one evening. One daughter played the flute and other the recorder.

On Tuesday afternoon the pastor took us to Bolahun to the Episcopal Holy Cross Mission. Besides Ginny's work we visited a leper colony nearby where we visited with a recent graduate of EBSN. He was a recovered leper working in the leper colony. In a field nearby, I counted fourteen different kinds of butterflies. Beautiful!

Thursday morning, we rode twenty miles to Foya, standing in the back of a pickup with twelve others. Here we were guests of Pastor Mueller and family, a Missouri Lutheran Pastor. We walked to the Swedish Pentecostal Mission Clinic and Health Center which was staffed only with nurses and midwives, with a doctor's visit once a month. Two years previously they had had a major outbreak of measles. They had only one case so far this year after emphasis on immunizations. Immunizations work!

On Good Friday morning we went to the small village of Taoma. Here we participated in a service where the Bible reading was read in a Kiese dialect. This was the first time they had heard the Bible read in their own language! What a thrill it was! We marched around from their outside church setting and around the cross, singing hymns in Kiese language. The Passion story was then read in their own dialect. How happy they were and what a privilege to be a participant! I'll not forget that experience. I recently received a plea from Wycliffe Translators that Indonesia had one hundred dialects to be translated into the Gospel. I had to respond! It's a miracle to hear the Living Word in language dear to you!

How many God Moments can you find?

RETURNING HOME

I returned home for the fourth of July 1986 for the Sunday church service. Jane, Paul, Ralph and I all wore our Liberian shirts and dresses. I had a warm welcome from my pastor and congregation. I remember singing the hymn with tears in my eyes: "This is my song, O God of all the nations, a song of peace for lands afar and mine. This is my home, the country where my heart is; here are my hopes, my dreams, my holy shrine; but other hearts in other lands are beating with hopes and dreams as true and high as mine." My world had grown to include Liberia. And I think also for my congregation.

They had posted a chart with every day of my six-month stay on the bulletin board with a space to contribute $10 a day for my expenses. Every spot was taken! One eight-year-old boy had saved up his allowance and supported me for one day! Not having to pay for apartment or utilities, that was adequate to cover my food, personal expenses and the travel I did within the country. Eating the local food most of the time, it was enough. For the Liberians I was still a rich American and they often asked for donations which I gave sparingly. They, after all, earned only $1 to $2 per day, if that. And their theme was, you have to ask! She might have money to give and if we don't ask, she won't have a chance to give it.

Generally, communication was a challenge. Many congregational members had written to me and I wrote a letter to the congregation one or two times a month. In March we arranged an Adult Forum on Sunday morning when, by telephone we talked together. I was at a telephone in Monrovia, they were at the educational hour on Sunday morning. The phone connection was very good. It was exciting for me and I know Pastor Eisele said that it was a highlight for him. Our mail service in Liberia was

15

only to the church office in Monrovia. It came to Zor Zor only when someone carried it up, every week or so. There was no phone service in our area. Dr. Munson had a shortwave radio that he used to communicate with the Monrovia church office and with church business in the USA as well as his personal use. He was generous to let others use it occasionally. Reception was often poor so not too dependable. My daughter Jane graduated from Concordia College in May. I tried to call her, but the line was too noisy. (Now I can Skype to Tanzania, Japan, New Zealand — talk and see their faces and surroundings.)

I was so blessed by this adventure. Especially important to me was to experience God's loving care. I had been doing my daily Bible studies for almost three years, hearing about God's love and care but this was experiencing it. My faith continued to grow and my relationship with God strengthened.

The congregation was also blessed. Through my experience they grew to know the blessings of mission work. We started by giving a scholarship to Kokulo, a member of the practical nursing class I taught. He was working on a bachelor's degree, so he could teach in the Esther Bacon School of Nursing. When the war broke out in 1990, he fled to Guinea and we lost contact. Eventually the congregation developed its mission program in Central America which continued for many years.

In the Grand Rapids community, I was asked to show my slide presentation and talk about my experience to many of the area organizations as well as school classes. It was wonderful for me because I could relive my experiences and witness to a wide audience.

I went back to work as a public health nurse September first. It was difficult fitting back into that role. As I read my journals, I realize how miserable I was. In Liberia the doctors were teasing me, maybe warning me, saying, "How are they going to keep her up in the woods, after she's been to Liberia?" And I was thinking that restlessness and discomfort was connected with reentry.

After about two months, two patients asked for a different nurse. I was having difficulty sleeping, I was irritable with highs and lows and extremely concerned about getting my work done as well as my marriage relationship. Finally, after six months I went to see a counselor. I remember that first time I went. I thought the whole world could see me going into that office and what would they think, me going to a counselor! That was a fleeting concern. After we had talked about my Liberian experience, I mentioned that I was an incest survivor. The counselor's facial expression changed. She excused herself for a couple of minutes and came back with some papers. She had been to a workshop recently on incest, she said, and had an informational booklet for incest survivors as well as a checklist. The checklist was to help me identify common problem areas associated with the trauma. I checked practically all on the list. How shocked I was at first. In time, I was so thankful!

Fourteen years earlier when I was director of the practical nursing program at the junior college, incest had reared its head. We were with the students at a psychiatric hospital and I inquired about recovery help. The therapists there were very sympathetic but knew of no program.

Again, in the spring before I went to Liberia, thirteen years later, I was looking for a therapist who could help me. At that time, I was doing a 50-Day-Adventure program. One of the disciplines was to pray each day, "I commit my life to you. If there is anything about me that needs to change, God, please change it." I came home from a Lenten service one night and was directed to talk to my pastor about the incest. I talked to him the next day. He told me I needed to forgive my father. I told him I didn't know how. He said, "Of course you do, you've been going to church all these years." He had a lot to learn about incest recovery, and I had a lot to learn about forgiveness. I searched for local resources that could help me and found none.

So, when I heard there was help, I was relieved. I would read the pamphlet and come back next week. Julie helped me a lot but after a couple of months she referred me to a more spiritually centered lady, Jackie, who could help me leave my burden of shame and guilt at the cross with Jesus.

I was in therapy off and on for the next four years. I was in a group that was very helpful for me. It was led by Jackie and another lady who had abuse experience and knowledge. She also seemed to have unresolved issues with her own anger. That was a big problem for me. I had lots of issues of my own: finding my feelings, learning how to use them appropriately, especially acceptable use of anger, dealing with shame and guilt, anger at my father, and the rejection by my mother during my father's incarceration and release from prison. This forced me from my parental home at sixteen.

Midway in this time I was introduced to Centering Prayer by Jackie. She formed an ecumenical group to practice the intention of sitting quietly before God called contemplative prayer. We met once a week as a group and as possible, practiced twice daily individually. I feel this was a great aid to my healing.

Where was God in all of this? I'm so thankful that God was with me. In looking back, I'm convinced that I needed the grounding in God that I found in the Bible Study and the experiences in Liberia. Without my relationship with God I don't think I would have been able to go through the therapy.

The God Moments for me were experiencing God in finding a therapist who had some background in incest recovery. I was thankful that she could refer me to Jackie who could connect it to my faith. She took me to a journey to the cross where I could dump shame. (Of course, not all of it dumped and disappeared that easily!) Jackie was such a blessing to me. And I saw God as I connected to the group and the wonderful women who I met there.

Are you going through a difficult time? Ask God to go with you, to guide you. And don't be afraid of counselors. They have been so helpful to me.

GOD REALLY IS EVERYWHERE

Of course, we've heard it many times but sometimes you have to experience it.

For Christmas 1987, Paul, my son, gave Ralph and me each enough travel points to go to Japan. We had hosted Makiko for a year, a Japanese AFS exchange student in 1980. She came back with her sister to visit since and I was excited for a chance to visit her. Paul was going to Japan for a business trip and then on to China. I said, "Maybe I could join you to go to China?" He thought about it and then invited me to meet him at Narita airport in Japan. We would go first to Hong Kong and on to China. Paul arranged for our visa and we made plans together.

As we were hiking on a trail in China, Paul was eager to move rapidly. I urged him on and sat on a bench, reflecting on where I was prayerfully. God was with me in Grand Rapids, Minnesota. I knew that. And certainly, God had been there in Liberia with me. Now, here I was in China and God was here. It's true! God is everywhere! It still amazes me as I think about it. God is so much more that we can ever imagine. God's love so much greater, God's compassion and care surrounds us and holds us. This was a special God Moment for me.

There were several others that I recall from that trip. We saw the Forbidden City, visited a Christian church, the Great Wall, Tiananmen Square where months later there was a massacre during a student revolt, and other sights in China. Paul went on to Korea and I to Tokyo. I took the bus from Narita airport into Tokyo. Makiko was now engaged to Hidiaki, and he was picking me up at the bus. He had written me a note and drew a picture of himself, a round face, slant eyes and a big shock of dark hair on a well-built frame, six foot, four inches tall. People on the bus were asking who was meeting me, and I explained. "You'll never find him since you don't know what he looks like," they said. When the bus pulled into the station, there was Hidiaki. He looked just like the picture and at 6' 4" soared high above the others. And he recognized me. We were all so surprised and happy.

When I was in Tokyo sightseeing with Makiko, we were passing shrines to the many different gods they worshipped. She stopped to toss a coin as a prayer in a fountain. I asked, "Makiko, who will answer your prayer?" "The dragon," she replied. Paul and I had observed the celebration of Chinese New Year in China, The Year of the Dragon. They made the dragons out of shiny paper. Makiko had heard of the Christian God at our house as she attended church with us regularly. Her parents were concerned that she would change her religion, so she was very guarded. How thankful I was that I knew a Living God that truly answered prayer.

Days later when I was visiting Makiko's family conversing as best we could without an interpreter, I understood that Makiko's older sister had attended a Catholic school. I said, "Oh, then she knows the Christian God." And her father said, "Missh-ion-ary." for they had heard of my work in Liberia. I started to deny and then said proudly, "Yes, I am a missionary. I want to share the 'Good News', how Jesus came to demonstrate love, to give his life for our salvation." I had not really accepted that as an identity until that moment.

I DON'T WANT TO CHANGE

I had been told by two counselors, when we discussed my marriage, "Someday you may want to look at that." I had been doing some self-study. I listened to tapes by Ernie Larson on topics, "Adult Children of Alcoholic and Dysfunctional Families," a series called, "Building Self Esteem," and his Spirituality Series. I read the book, Codependent No More by Melody Beattie I learned that the example I saw in my home of codependence was something I had adopted and needed to work on. It wasn't the woman's duty to make her man happy. I became aware that I had fully accepted that as my responsibility. And Ralph wasn't happy, particularly if I was. If I got excited about something, he would pull away with a dour countenance. His pulling away left me feeling guilty as well as rejected again.

I told Ralph how unhappy I was. I felt his distancing as rejection. At work I had a lot of pressure with inadequate time to do my charting and Medicare forms with little understanding from my supervisor. I asked Ralph to go with me to a counselor. After some time, he agreed to go with me to the woman I'd been seeing. She asked him questions and he just sat there quietly, saying nothing. She asked him to tell her he couldn't answer, and he said nothing. When it was my turn, I expressed my frustration with feeling so distant to him while longing for intimacy. When asked for his perception, he did not contribute to the conversation. I left the session feeling so sorry for him.

But the situation didn't change for me. I remember being at work in the Fall of 1988 when I had what felt like a large burning ball in my chest. I just couldn't go on like this. I asked for a week of vacation, called for a reservation at a Catholic retreat center and told Ralph I was going away for a week of quiet.

It was a time of simple Centering Prayer twice a day, conference time with a Sister daily. I did readings from their library, maybe a nap or a walk in the brisk autumn air and one day we had group worship. It was good. Ralph called on Wednesday saying he and Lars, our dog, missed me.

When I came home on Friday we went out for dinner and talked about my experience. I told him I needed more from him. He was mostly silent. He said he was lonely when I was gone. I said I thought we needed a counselor to help us work this out. I suggested we not go back to the lady we had seen but go to a man. He didn't express his opinion.

I hadn't unpacked my suitcase. I took it to the downstairs bedroom and that night slept there. I made a decision that night. If Ralph was unwilling to go to counseling, I, who could never imagine I would get divorced, decided I would have to leave him. The next morning Ralph agreed to go to counseling. (A God Moment)

We went to a male counselor. Briefly into the first session, the counselor asked me to wait in the waiting room. Afterwards Ralph told me the counselor told him to tell me that he was angry that I left him to go to Liberia. He didn't ever want me to do that again. I said I was sorry he was hurt. I also said I had hoped he would come with me — I was dreaming about doing more Third World volunteering and hoped we could do it together. At a later time, we talked about retirement. He said he wanted to work on his tree farm. I told him I wanted to do short term mission work and between, help him on the tree farm.

We went to this counselor five or six times. The counselor said he saw me pulling at Ralph to get close and Ralph pulling away. During the next several months I saw Ralph trying to allow me closer, then pull away. He tried to share his ideas and world view with me a time or two. Then pull back. He probably gave it his best effort. Things really had not changed for me.

In June we had an appointment with a different male counselor in Duluth. He had only two weeks before he was taking a lengthy vacation. During the first session he interviewed us separately. The second session was on our thirty-first wedding anniversary, June fifteenth. The counselor summarized what I had told him. I said I felt I needed some change in our relationship. And Ralph had his say. He said he was happy with who he was. He didn't want to change and didn't see that it was needed. The counselor affirmed that we all get to decide who we want to be and the course in life we want to follow. At the end he wished us well in working this out.

This was a clear God Moment for me. Ralph had no interest in changing. I was the one who was changing expectations. I couldn't live with our relationship the way it was. I prayed. What would I do? I would have to move? Where would I go? I had a dream of finding a place on a lake.

I started to say my good-byes. To the walks by the river. To my house. What a wonderful house it was! Small but with three bedrooms on the main floor and one in the basement. We had a nice living room with a fireplace. I had put a sliding door to replace the large window in the living room, accessing the patio and flower bed in the backyard just the year before. I was saying good-by to the neighborhood and neighbors I had lived near for thirty years. Many tears.

I started to look at available apartments. Not too interesting. I asked my coworkers. One said, "Talk to Kate. She might know of one." A week later I had found nothing. I mentioned it again at work. The same coworker said, "Have you talked to Kate?" I hadn't. She worked part time and wasn't around the office, but now I called her. Her relative had an apartment that was never advertised, and she would check to see if it was available. It was available! Another God Moment! It was on McKinney Lake, in town. I could look at it the next lunch hour.

What a blessing! A roomy one-bedroom basement apartment with walkout to the lake, thirty feet out the door. Not advertised as the main entrance required walking through the home of a 90-year-old woman with a full-time caretaker. There was a canoe that I could use, and a swimming beach. It was partially furnished but I could bring my own furniture. It was available July first.

Chris and Bill and Jane were home for July fourth weekend. I asked Ralph if I could use his pickup to move and he reluctantly agreed. I asked my girls if they would help me. They were hesitant. I assured them that I would move, and it would help me a great deal if they would assist me. They finally agreed. We moved a few pieces of furniture and my personal items.

This was a wonderful place to heal. Now I could seriously work on the abuse trauma as I was beginning to work on my issues in a group. I lived there two years. I experienced the freezing over of the lake with a dramatic scene of the otter climbing from the water to the ice over and again one winter day. I enjoyed seeing the loons nest and parent their two babies who grew into full sized adults. I experienced swimming one day when the mother dove under the water, headed my way. I had never been attacked by a mother loon and I didn't want to. I got out of the lake! I fished from the canoe and caught some fish! And one spring day as I returned from work, I joined the celebration of the opening of the lake. The wind was blowing the ice to one side. The birds were flying around singing. The

25

loons joined the chorus. I don't know who else was there but what a joyous occasion! I loved living on the lake. God moments were there. Where have you experienced yours?

I had prayed that we could reconcile and get back together. I saw Ralph occasionally. We went out to dinner. There was no meaningful discussion. In early December when talking to my pastor, he told me, "Why don't you leave Ralph alone and let him work this out for himself." I would do that. I talked to a lawyer about divorce. He explained the details about how property and assets would be divided. I took a friend with me to the house and gathered what I wanted from the linen closet and the cupboards. I talked to Ralph about the furniture I wanted to take and arranged a moving truck to move them to my apartment. I felt I was fair. As usual, he said little or nothing. But he was upset. I was very sad.

Before I went to Liberia, I selected the Bible verse, Psalm 32:8 as my guide. It says, *"I will instruct you and teach you the way you should go; I will counsel you with my eye upon you."* I felt God's guidance and counsel.

My Christian counselor and I had prayed together and I separately with great confidence for Ralph and my marriage to be healed. This wasn't the healing I had desired, but I believed God was with me. So, I moved on.

HELP ME! HELP ME!

Mom was having a hard time. I had a call from my sister. If I wanted to see Mom alive, I should come. It was Friday afternoon. At first, I wondered if I wanted to see her. But I quickly packed my suitcase after work and started the five-hour road trip. I arrived at the care center about 11:30 PM expecting to stop, say hello and go on to my sister's house. As I walked into her room, I saw her — arms extended, sitting up, crying: "Help Me! Help Me!"

There was no anger. I hugged her, told her who I was, reassured her. I was confident she knew me but was unable to reply. Her arms were tight around my neck. She clung to me.

I had last seen her three weeks ago when she was admitted to the care center. The past year had been difficult for her. In March she had been hospitalized because of heart block, resulting from a buildup of her heart medicine, Lanoxin. She was ninety-one years old and that sometimes happens just because the kidneys are unable to clear it. I came then, wondering if the doctors were prolonging her life but found she was very urgently wanting to get well. She seemed to be strongly hanging on to life.

She had been managing quite well. She lived alone in her house with some assistance from my sister, Jeanette, who lived in the area. My brother, Earl, was also nearby but not very involved. The rest of us were scattered. Arline in Sleepy Eye, Dorothy in St. Paul, me in Grand Rapids, all in Minnesota. Georgia lived in Seattle, Washington and Laverne in Boise, Idaho.

Since Mom had six daughters, she had expressed in my hearing that surely one of us would take care of her. She wouldn't have to go into a care center. But in the last year, Jeanette's husband had a massive stroke

27

and she was now his caregiver. During the summer and fall Laverne had come to visit. She had a job and a husband and son to get back to. Georgia and Dorothy came but neither could stay. I offered to bring her to Grand Rapids — she wasn't interested in that. So, Arline, now retired, came, and Conrad, her husband, joined her in the fall.

Mom's sunny personality was changing to one who was critical and demanding. I'm sure she was uncomfortable. She was sleeping poorly, needing help to toilet during the night. Her appetite was decreasing as food no longer appealed to her. She needed twenty-four-hour care.

Arline explored trying to find a live-in caregiver in the community and was unable to find anyone. With a history of mental health issues and Mom's change in personality, Arline's health began to decline. They decided to take New Year's weekend off and I would stay with Mom. Arline saw her doctor back home and he recommended she not care for her mother any longer. "You'll never get well if you continue there," he advised her. So, she would not return.

I had a full-time job as a Public Health Nurse in Grand Rapids. Mom refused to come there with me. I had been separated from Ralph for six months and I needed to work to support myself. I was still in incest therapy, and Mom's personality change made it difficult for me to care for her, also. I talked to my sisters on the phone. None were available to come. They agreed that Mom needed to go to the care center in Morris.

I tried to talk to Mom about the situation. She recognized that she needed help. I told her Arline tried to find live in-help and found none. The three-day weekend was coming to an end and I needed to return to Grand Rapids. She was not willing to come with me. Neither did she want to go to the care center. I called Earl, my brother, and asked for his assistance. He came in and told her she had to go, and she was cooperative but not

28

happy. (She was trained to listen to men.) She was admitted to the hospital that morning. I came to see her that evening. The nurse told me she had shoved her supper tray onto the floor, breaking the dishes. She wouldn't talk to me and while I was trying to visit with no response, her granddaughter came, and she smiled at her and had a conversation, completely ignoring me. She was angry. This was not the mother I knew. Her rejection hit me, and I became angry too.

I returned the next morning to more of the same treatment. I told her I was sorry that I couldn't stay and care for her. She was discharged, and I took her to the care center and helped with her admission and tried to help her settle in there. I assured her that Jeanette, Earl and her grandchildren would visit and would look out for her. Then I left for Grand Rapids.

And now she was here and calling for help. I asked Mom what was bothering her. She was unable to answer. I thought she was semi-comatose. Maybe she just didn't want to answer. I stayed that night, talking to her at times, dozing in the recliner at her bedside now and then. She responded warmly to my hugs.

In the morning I went to Jeanette's home, slept a few hours and returned late forenoon. I found a copy of the service book we used in Sunday School, years ago by the piano. I used this and read Scripture readings from it and sang those familiar hymns that she knew so well. She had taught Sunday School for years — we had used this book every Sunday. "I know Mom, that you know and believe that Jesus came to save us from our sins, how He suffered and died on the cross. He died there! The disciples were confused. They thought it was all lost, but on the third day, the tomb was empty. Jesus appeared to Mary, and later that day, he appeared to the disciples. They saw his wounds in his hands and the stab wound on his side. Jesus was alive! He had risen from the dead, securing

29

for us life eternal. You know that, don't you Mom? So, we don't have to be afraid of death. We can look forward to going to heaven." I talked to her about heaven — how wonderful it would be to see Jesus! To see him face to face! She'd see all the people who had already gone to heaven. They would have a great celebration when she arrived. I talked about all the people she would see there — her parents, her sisters, Pa — they would be waiting for her. And that little baby she had miscarried. Would she be grown up? Maybe still a baby. Heaven, a wonderful place with no tears, no stress and most important, there with Jesus.

I prayed with her for forgiveness of all her and my sins. I assured her God had forgiven her according to his promise. Then I told her she needed to forgive herself. I said I forgave her for not being able to stop the abuse, all of us girls did. Mom and I had had conversation about her part in the abuse. She had accepted no responsibility for that. I thought her struggle might be that she was feeling guilty and afraid to meet Jesus. I thought she wasn't ready to die. I read lots of Scripture passages and sang many hymns to her.

In my ministry I had a sermon where I told the story of her crying out, "Help Me! Help Me!" that emphasized that we all need to be ready so when our time comes, we won't be struggling.

I talked to my sister, Laverne, about this recently. She told me when she visited Mom that fall, she had talked to Mom about dying. Mom picked out Scripture and hymns for her funeral. Laverne asked her if she was afraid to die and she said she wasn't. Maybe Mom was ready. Maybe she wasn't afraid but lonely — just needing her family, someone to be with her.

I was there Saturday afternoon and night. Before I returned on Sunday, late morning, we had a call from the nurse at Jeanette's. The nurse said

Mom was running a fever and wondered if I was coming. I said I would soon be there. Jeanette and I didn't think we should treat her. I called Earl, and he wanted us to call the doctor and get treatment. The doctor ordered one dose of an antibiotic.

It was Sunday afternoon and I was considering returning to work on Monday. I realized that if I left, Mom would die alone. I couldn't leave her. I continued my schedule. The pastor visited on Tuesday afternoon with communion. Mom was calm. It's interesting that I can't remember having any conversation with Mom during those four nights and days I was there with her. I remember only her clinging to me so desperately and her call for help that first night.

On Tuesday evening we planned that I would come to Jeanette's to stay with her husband and she would visit Mom for a while. Shortly after she arrived, Mom's respirations changed. Jeanette read Psalm 91. As she was reading verses 9-12:

"Because you have made the Lord your refuge, the Most High your dwelling place,

No evil shall befall you, no scourge come near your tent.

For he will command his angels concerning you to guard you in all your ways.

On their hands they will bear you up."

Mom took her last deep breath.

What a beautiful ending. She went in the hands of the angels bearing her up.

The funeral was planned. The family gathered, and she was laid to rest. The next day the seven of us divided up the household goods. Some remained behind to help clean out the house. I returned to Grand Rapids that day.

All through this time with Mom, the feeling that I must file for divorce was strongly on my mind. Shortly after I returned, I filed for divorce. Ralph didn't want a divorce, nor did he want to make any changes himself. I thought we had worked out the financial agreement but in August my lawyer told me Ralph wanted to add a clause that he if needed to, he could come to me for money. I declined that request and we went to a court hearing in September. The divorce was granted September 28,1990 with no dependent clause. By that time, I was already working on plans for my future.

The God moment for me was seeing my Mom struggling, afraid. God gave me the words, the tools to calm her fears so she was ready to go to meet her Savior. And wasn't that a God Moment also that she took her last breath as Jeanette read the Scripture that the Angels' hands would lift her up to heaven?

SECTION II
SEMINARY

WHEN THE FULLNESS OF TIME CAME, GOD CALLED

Spirit Song

O let the Son of God enfold you with his Spirit and his love.
Let him fill your heart and satisfy your soul.
O let him have the things that hold you,
And his Spirit like a dove will descend upon your life and make you whole.
Jesus, O Jesus, come and fill your lambs.
Jesus, O Jesus, come and fill your lambs. (Mercy Publishing, 1979)

It was Pentecost Sunday when we celebrate the birth of the Christian Church as the Holy Spirit descends on the Christian community as recorded in Acts Chapter 2. In the Bible account, the Spirit came as a roaring wind with flame-like appearances on each person, enabling them to speak in a foreign language. Pastor Susan's sermon was about the Holy Spirit and the Wind. She talked about riding a bike. When you go one direction, the wind is in your face and as you turn around and go the other, it's still in your face. Wind is not always pleasant. It bucks against us. Like the wind, the Spirit is not always pleasant or expected. It's not offered; it's given. We must accept it! Sherri sang "Spirit Song." The words of the song along with the sermon flooded my being as I returned to my apartment.

It was a cool, cloudy, drizzly June day as I started on my walk that afternoon. But my heart was warmed as I thought of the church service. I had my plate full. My mother had died just a few months earlier. I was dealing with a pending divorce, having separated from Ralph nearly a year ago. Often, I would break out in tears missing him, causing rifts within my family, and missing my house. How could it be that our 32-year marriage

34

was ended? All my relationships were changed. I was angry. I was sad. And I was lonely.

I felt the wind in my face as I walked along. I was restless in my work as a Public Health Nurse. I had gone to Minneapolis and interviewed for several nursing positions there. I knew I couldn't move until the divorce was completed, so changing location wasn't an immediate option. And those jobs didn't sound very interesting anyway. The damp wind on my face reminded me of the Holy Spirit. And I prayed, "God, I don't know what to do? You are in this with me and are guiding my way. Just tell me what you want me to do! Even if I've never thought of it before, I'll do it! Lord, fill me with your Spirit. It may be surprising, I may not like it, but here I am."

It was a long walk, all around Ice Lake. I left my concerns about my future in the hands of God. I just enjoyed the fresh air, the green grass, the sounds and sights from the lake, and the spring breeze in my face.

When I got back to my apartment, I was a bit out of breath. So, I made a cup of tea and sat down by my table. There at my fingertips was a *Faith at Work* magazine. I'd already read it so I was just leafing through and stopped on an article by a woman, who at age sixty, had quit her teaching position to go to seminary in St. Louis. She had been teaching Junior High school students for years, taking courses at the seminary for her personal enrichment and conducting workshops on rational decision making in the summers. When she evaluated her seminary experience, she found that going full time for one year she could complete the requirements for a Master of Divinity degree. She was amazed and was led to follow that path. In writing this article she loudly exclaimed, "This is not a rational decision, but following the Spirit's leading is not always rational!"

Reading this article had a new meaning. I had this tingling feeling. God was right here! Answering my prayer. My first response was, "Take your time, God. You don't have to answer my prayer today!" But there it was. In that article I heard, "Margie, you go to seminary. That's what I want you to do!"

As I thought about it, I got this strange feeling — Filled. Then I thought, "I had been wishing Jane, my daughter, would go to seminary. Maybe it's me God wants there." What would I do with that? It would take me four years — if I went now when I'm 61, I'd be 65 when I finished. Starting a new career at 65? Mission work? Then I reflected on a pastor's comment, "Why are all these divorced women in the seminary, anyway?" Maybe because they couldn't hear the call when they were married. Perhaps there are a lot of divorced people out there who need ministering to. For sure, I don't know, God. This is amazing! Surprise? Absolutely! It sounded exciting — learn to preach, be able to administer the Lord's Supper, counsel as a pastor. The doctors in Liberia jokingly said to me, "How are they going to keep her out in the woods, after she's been to Liberia?" Thank you, God for answering my prayer. This just about blows me away!

The next day I had lunch with Pastor Susan. As she listened to my story, she expressed her support and surprise, and then told me that going to the seminary didn't mean I had to be ordained. We talked about our concerns: the 4-year course, the expense, getting a call at age 65. She would work with me.

Several years earlier when I went to Liberia on short term mission trip, I was led and strengthened by the verses in Psalm 32: 8-9, *"I will instruct you and teach you the way you should go; I will counsel you with my eye upon you. Do not be like a horse or a mule, without understanding whose temper must be curbed with bit and bridle, else it will not stay near you."*

God had led me before. Took me to Liberia as I learned to trust and rely on God's wonderful promises and direction. I knew I could put myself under God's counsel and instruction. But to Seminary at age 61?

That weekend I visited my daughter Jane who was planning a wedding in two months. Her intended, Peter, suggested that perhaps Bethany Fellowship program would be a possibility as their course was two years instead of four. I was somewhat familiar with Bethany Fellowship's program. Two of my Fairview nursing classmates had been trained as missionaries there. Interestingly, that next day there was an article in the Sunday paper about Bethany's history and program.

When I stopped at the church the next week to get an application for the Global Mission Event (GME), I had a brief visit with Pastor Susan. She asked me if there was anything new. I mentioned Peter's suggestion of the Bethany Fellowship Program as a possibility. Did she look relieved? She encouraged me to look at this as a process. I would need to look into retirement options, talk to someone at Luther Seminary and Bethany, and share with our senior pastor. Now I was looking forward to the GME in about three weeks where I would have a chance to visit with Harold Hanson, who had helped facilitate my mission experience in Liberia.

Lord I want to be open to your Spirit. Blow into me. Enlighten me. Help me to be patient.

ON THE WAY

Carlene was a friend that I had grown very fond of in the last several years. It was when her youngest daughter, Karen was killed in a car accident that we became close friends.

What a shock! Her lovely 18-year-old Karen was riding in the back seat of sister's car, seat belt on. Three of them were going from Grand Rapids to Minneapolis on a Sunday morning when they were hit by a drunken driver, and Karen was killed immediately.

We spent time walking, talking, drinking tea, sharing our concerns and even a Faith at Work workshop in La Cross, Wisconsin three years before. We were both on renewed spiritual journeys, and God's love for each of us was the center of caring for one another.

And here we were traveling to the Global Mission Event (GME) at Carthage College in Kenosha — I, Carlene, and her granddaughter.

I was introduced to GME when I returned from Liberia in 1986. My church offered to send me that year, and I'd gone every year since. And what a blessing it was to me. There was a wonderful mission centered program for four days of preaching, learning new international hymns, and mini sessions on global ministry throughout the world. Equally important was getting reconnected with missionaries from Liberia and making new friends as well as renewing old ones. But for this trip, I had one main goal. I wanted to speak with Harold Hanson, the man who had helped me connect with Liberia. Since I had returned from my missionary experience at Curran Hospital teaching nursing, I had thought my retirement would be dedicated to doing short-term missionary work. I hoped Mr. Hanson would be able to help me figure out how that would blend with my recent call to seminary.

It was a busy time. Carlene and her granddaughter made their schedule, and I had mine. I saw Harold around the campus and understood that he was orienting new missionaries at this event. He was scheduled to conduct a session for those interested in volunteering for short term missionary work, and I decided to attend that to connect with him one to one.

When I arrived for that session, I found that I was his only participant! I was apologizing to him, thinking he wouldn't have any candidates for short term ministry while Harold was reassuring me that God intended that we have this time to talk. We spent that hour together discussing my impending divorce, my call to seminary, and my expectation to do short term ministry after I retired. When we finished, I thought I would go to seminary for one year and apply to teach English as a second language in China. That assignment paid a stipend and would alleviate concerns about finances. I received a caring, concerned, grace filled experience blessing me on my way.

My next step was contacting the seminaries. Luther, Wartburg, and Lutheran School of Theology in my area were sent letters of inquiry. On August fifteenth while in St. Paul, I had an interview at Luther Seminary. I wondered what kind of reception I would receive. The counselor was so kind, telling me it was never too late to study. It didn't mean that I would have to be ordained. I mentioned my conversation with Mr. Hanson and the idea that I would study for one year and do short term ministry. He talked about possibly starting a MA program and finishing it at a later time.

I remember him explaining that God's directions could be like the headlights on a car at night, showing us a small patch of the road, not the total picture. He encouraged me to be patient, suggesting that I ask others what I do well and asking their opinions.

Visiting on August 15, it was the day of the Festival of Mary, the Mother of our Lord. The chapel sermon was given by the Dean of Students, a woman, who centered on Mary's life of service. It left me feeling that I was on the right track. Going to seminary in my sixties was all right.

My divorce was final in September.

My next seminary visit was scheduled for October. A pastor friend who graduated from Lutheran School of Theology in Chicago and worked at Luther Seminary thought Wartburg might be a good fit for me. I planned a long weekend, going to Wartburg in Dubuque, Iowa on Friday and an old friend's daughter's wedding on Saturday in Decorah.

My dear co-worker's husband had died unexpectedly, so at the beginning of the trip, I headed north to Virginia, Minnesota. Since I would miss his funeral, I wanted to visit her as it was so unexpected. I left there for Dubuque in a somber mood.

As I was interested in diversity, I heard about Dubuque's history with African Americans. Being on the Mississippi River, they often had African Americans wanting to get off the boats to live in Dubuque. There was an organized movement that forced them to stay on the boat, and they gave them money to continue their journey up stream. In the recent past there had been a cross-burning on an African American's front yard. The seminary hosted a sizable group of foreign students without problem.

The women I spoke with told of the supportive staff and the adjustment to full time studies extending into night hours. The Pastoral Care Professor was especially kind in asking about my recent divorce — so much so that I started crying. Like a dam breaking, I couldn't stop the tears. I sniffled through the rest of the interview, went to my room, and cried and cried.

I came to realize I had not taken time to grieve my mother's death in

January or my divorce in September. Faced with a long ride to Iowa, my friend's grief, and a sympathetic professor, it all came out. I learned that grief was demanding attention.

At the wedding the next day, the bride, daughter of a classmate, apartment mate and dear friend who had died several years before, honored her mother with a single rose. It was a lovely celebration.

IT'S CRAZY

The social hour after church each Sunday was such a special time. Here I visited with other members, some long-time friends offering support to each other, some building relationships with others different from me. This is where I'd come to know a couple who had moved to our area to be near their son and grandchildren. He had been in an administrative position at a large corporation in the city. Retiring at age fifty-five, they relocated to a town of 8,000.

This Sunday, as I was visiting with them, I shared that I was making plans to go to the seminary. Their expressions of surprise and disbelief shocked me. I left thinking that what I was planning sounded crazy! Maybe I was wrong. It helped me realize that what was beginning to seem reasonable to me didn't look that way to others. Considering their expressions, even crazy!

After I had lunch, I called my friend Gerri. What a wonderful support she was for me. In talking with her about what I was planning to do, quit my public health nursing job and start a new career in seminary, it didn't sound rational. I told her about my experience at church and how I was doubting that going to seminary was the right thing to do. It made me feel like it was a crazy idea. "It is crazy," she said, "but it's all right." Gerri had heard of my call, and although she was reassuring, it left me feeling doubtful as I hung up the phone.

It was a cold winter day, and the apartment was chilly. I always enjoyed the warmth of a fire in the fireplace so carefully arranged the logs and started a blazing fire. It snapped and crackled as it threw off sparks. I stood there thinking about going to school for four years. I cried, "God, why do I have to go to seminary? I have lots of skills I can use for you?"

The message I heard as I was looking into that fire was, "This is for you. I want you to experience my grace. You have been working all these years. You have been earning and supporting your family. Now I want you to do this to receive from me."

My! What a God! That answer was right there! I'd never heard a voice from God and was amazed that God would answer my question. It seemed like the voice came out of my center — kind of knowing that Jesus lives in me. Perhaps that's not so remarkable, but it is! When we open our lives to Jesus, I believe that Jesus lives in our hearts. He lives in me. Jesus is **alive** in me!

What I heard that day was that this was for me! That was incredible — Jesus cared enough about me to plan this for me, to reassure me! Yes, I was learning that I was important to God. A personal relationship was what God desired for me. I wrote the rest in my journal but didn't remember it. I only reviewed it recently and was surprised. I guess receiving God's gift of grace wasn't in my understanding at that time. That calling me apart to be blessed with God's guidance and provision helped me to grow in my faith and prepared me for ordained ministry. This call wasn't to work and busyness. God wanted me to turn my life over, learn to trust, learn to obey. I was to continue my journey by resting in Jesus, my Savior. But school didn't sound like resting. It sounded like plenty of work. I was reassured that God was leading me.

I had struggled with writing the essay for my admission application to Wartburg and Luther Seminaries. So much so that I felt I had to get away to do it. My son gave me a plane ticket in December, and I spent a week at a motel in Sanibel, Florida by the sea, quiet, finding the words to describe my journey including incest recovery and divorce. Luther's response to my application for admission was a letter stating their requirement of an

43

interview with the Dean of Students for anyone who had been divorced. My appointment was the following week. I had been uneasy about this, but reassured by my recent experience before the fireplace, I found no need for nervousness. The woman dean was so gracious and understanding, affirming my call. When asked, she assured me that negativism toward divorced students had improved a great deal, although it might be encountered occasionally.

When I had opportunity to visit classes, my guide was delayed in getting me to a classroom of a highly acclaimed professor. I was left at the front entrance of the room and quietly walked in to take the nearest seat. The professor interrupted his lecture to ask me to move to the back row as I was a visitor. I slunk, red-faced to a proper seat in the back row.

But I enjoyed the content of the class — the stimulation and the process of learning again! I would enjoy the academic atmosphere. Speaking with women students later, I heard them struggling to meet deadlines. One told me of staying up all night to finish a paper. I vowed to myself never to do that.

Housing for single students was a room in the dorm, meals in the cafeteria which was closed on weekends. How would that work for me?

The Dean from Wartburg phoned me following my application. He was wondering if I was ready to begin a program of study. I understood, based on my grief meltdown when I was there. I apologized again, explaining my situation and assuring him I felt I was ready and would like to spend one-year emphasizing mission work. He informed me their mission professor would be on sabbatical for six months the following year. That was an unexpected message. I thanked him for the information.

THE SEARCH GOES ON

"Go to Pacific Lutheran Seminary in Berkeley, California," my brother-in-law said as we talked on the phone. I was telling him about my preference for Wartburg but found their mission professor would be on sabbatical for six months of the year, and my hesitancy about Luther. He had graduated from Pacific Lutheran many years earlier. I contacted them and received their material. A couple of weeks later, a postcard from the president with a lovely scene of the Pacific Ocean urging me to consider their seminary. California was far away from support. I wasn't sure I was ready for that.

I had been journaling for years, so I prayerfully made a list in my journal of the characteristics I would like to find in a seminary. Within a week I received a letter from Lutheran School of Theology in Chicago. I had written a letter to them initially stating my interests and received a form letter with their brochure. The form letter didn't speak to my interests, so I put it in my file. But this new letter was different. It stated that I had inquired, and they hadn't heard from me. This letter was telling me what they offered. And what they offered almost exactly followed what I had journaled I was looking for! I compared the two lists. I couldn't believe it! I would have to look at this.

My son, who lives in Chicago, offered a plane ticket one way and his second car to drive back to store in his father's garage until fall. I came the first weekend in May. It was south of Grand Rapids, so I thought it would be warm. But no, it was Chicago — windy, damp, cool. I had a full day scheduled with class visits to Old Testament Prophets by the Dean. When he started the class with prayer, that was a first, and I was impressed. Then I attended chapel service, reformation history class, and had an appointment with the mission professor. It was a very good visit. I had strong encouragement from the president and the mission professor to come to Chicago. Housing was offered in apartments on campus, built for the World's Fair one hundred years ago, but very pleasant.

Yes, it was very positive, but it also raised a few concerns. I'd heard it before but was asked again. What did my Synod Committee think about my aspirations? Maybe now was the time to find out. I called for an appointment. I had talked about my experience with Centering Prayer. This caused concerns about my being a mystic, and the church hierarchy was afraid of mysticism. I didn't feel like a mystic, but I'd certainly been blessed by Centering Prayer.

The Synod Seminary Committee, with the seminary's help, approved candidates after one year of study for the Master of Divinity program. At this time in history, they rarely met with the candidates until that time. So, when I met with this committee, these members had never met with someone before they started seminary. Although women at various ages had been going to seminary for twenty years, my interest at the age of sixty was unusual. I met with three pastors. Why did I wat to go to seminary? I shared about my call but couldn't articulate why I wanted to go nor why I was excited to attend classes other than I wanted to study the Bible and theology. Why couldn't I just go and get a job? I could send my resume to the bishops and get a job right now, they said. I wanted to go to seminary. One pastor didn't think I should change anything for five years because it took five years to heal after a divorce. They thought I was immature because I didn't know exactly what I wanted to do. Another said I shouldn't go into ministry unless there was absolutely nothing else I could do. After the two-hour session, I was advised not to go to seminary. It was too hard (I might not pass), it was too expensive, it was too long, and the church wouldn't get its investment out of me as the church helped support the seminary education.

Needless to say, I was devastated. I was crying so hard I could hardly drive as I left. I stopped at the mall and shopped for a while to calm myself before the eighty-mile drive home. I retired the red and white striped shirt I bought that day just last year! (twenty-seven years later)

I had some praying and thinking to do. First of all, I knew I didn't need that committee's permission to go to seminary. Anyone could go as a special student for a year. Secondly, I had prayed telling God that whatever God led me to do, I'd do it, even if I hadn't thought of it before. I felt the call was strong. It was unusual. It was unexpected. And, I had that voice tell me in front of the blazing fireplace that God wanted me to go to seminary. How could they tell me not to go? I prayed about this. Thirdly, I wanted to go to seminary. It was uplifting to visit those classes. I enjoyed going to school. I wanted to study the Bible. I wasn't worried about passing the classes. I had been valedictorian of my high school class. I wasn't concerned about money. I would have a pension and soon Social Security, and I could find the money — even work part time as a nurse if necessary. And as for being a responsible steward of the church's investment in me, I would follow God's calling and direction. It wasn't the church I was interested in pleasing as much as it was my God.

In the discussion, there was a suggestion that I take a Clinical Pastoral Education (CPE) course before I go to seminary. This was part of the curriculum for a MDiv program and usually done after the first year of seminary. This program was offered at St. Mary's Hospital in Duluth. I made an appointment with a teacher in the program. After hearing some of my story, she asked me, "What would make you feel good? You have been through a lot of trauma, so many things that have been hurtful and upsetting. What would make you feel good? Do what you would like to do." This was grace — undeserved and unconstrained divine favor. It was a gift from God; God's loving mercy for me coming in the words of this beautiful CPE supervisor. Thank you, Jesus. I so appreciated those words. I came to know that I wanted to go to seminary.

A few days later I wrote a thank you letter to the committee and the bishop saying I would enter Lutheran School of Theology as a special student in September. I was going because I felt called to seminary, I wanted to go, and I was excited to join in studying the Bible and Theology. The bishop responded with a letter of encouragement.

TRANSITION TO SEMINARY

It was sad leaving Grand Rapids. I moved there newly married after my husband had secured employment with the Department of Natural Resources thirty-three years earlier. We found meaningful employment, had eventually bought a home, raised our family, and participated in the community and church activities. After we separated, I lived for the past two years in an apartment a few feet from a lake. What a peaceful place.

There had been the retirement party hosted by my coworkers for family and friends where we laughed a lot as we wore blue painted paper hats made out of newspaper. You see I had a beautiful skipper blue hat that I had worn on home visits the last year. Ginger and Sherry sang "Friends Forever" as the tears formed in my eyes. Friends, Mary and Gerry, did their skit of "Ole and Lena." With final efforts to clean out all the kitchen cupboards asking, "And what do we do with this?" the U-Haul was now packed with furniture and my too many (50) boxes. Wonderful friends Gerri, Russ and Mary and Gale were so helpful. My sister Dorothy was also a part of the packing.

Russ had generously offered to drive the truck while I would follow with the car, first to St. Paul, and then on to Chicago the next morning. At a last check through the apartment, I found pinned on the curtain in the bedroom a little rabbit which was made by my mother in a craft session. Just a little cotton ball with eyes, nose, and little pink ears. I unpinned it and put it in my car. It rode along with me, above the mirror. This finding was such an emotional ending — a signal to me that God was reminding me of his concern by connecting me to my mother and was going along with me. My sister, riding with me back her home in St. Paul, wondered why I was crying. I was overwhelmed by God's love. I was missing my mom, sad to leave my friends and the familiar, excited about my new adventure, and yet feeling a little fearful. But the presence of that small rabbit gave me comfort and reassurance. And, yes, it still rides with me in my car.

I wondered how to make that transition — from living on a lake in a small town to an apartment in the city. I had asked the dean of students. He referred me to a picture of a lake on his office wall. "That is where I like to be," he said. "That picture is taken from my cabin in up-state New York where I go as often as I can. Here in Chicago, I go to Lake Michigan. It's a nice walk which gives me space and refreshment."

My friend, Gale, had written in a card, "Find beauty where you can." She and I had been prayer partners, well sort of — she was busy with personal issues as well as taking classes at the junior college. I was hoping I could find a prayer partner at seminary.

My first Sunday in Chicago, I was invited by a Chinese student to attend a mixed culture church. The congregation was predominately African American. We were invited to stay for coffee which really was lunch. As we sat at the table, one of the women asked if I'd be interested in being a prayer partner. One of their members had recently moved away and their group of four had an open spot. They prayed on the phone Monday through Friday at 6 AM. I was amazed! This was an African-American woman who I met only minutes before, inviting me to join her prayer group — having three prayer partners, not one. But 6AM! I'm not a morning person. Cautious me, I took her phone number, prayed about it, and accepted a few days later. Praying with these women, my prayer partners, was a very rich experience for me. All three ladies were Black. They shared their struggles with me, and I shared mine with them. I was so thankful that God had provided me with this experience. On Christmas break, I invited them to lunch, so we could meet. What a fun time we had! They brought flowers and a Christmas card. The card was addressed, "Margie White." We all got a chuckle out of that. They were so surprised to find that wasn't really my name. They prayed me through seminary starting from the first day! What a gift.

I had a pleasant one-bedroom apartment with big windows, high ceilings, and white walls! How bright it was, especially after living in a basement apartment with dark paneling for two years! There were new friends to make and many challenges ahead. One morning as I was preparing my breakfast, I was serenaded by a wren singing from the branch of the tree just outside my kitchen window. "Find beauty where you can." Thank you, Gale and God for this reminder.

Lake Michigan was about a fifteen-minute walk, about a mile. I walked there often. Sometimes with friends. We picnicked there. But often I came alone, watched people swim, looked at the blue water and watched the small waves lap on the shore, and exercised or relaxed. In the winter, I went to observe the piles of ice build-up. Before I left Chicago, I found a large photograph of Lake Michigan which has hung in my study ever since.

USE WHAT YOU HAVE

Sunday morning was bright and crisp. I went to the parking lot for my car, ready to drive the five miles to the African American church I attended to do my Contextual Education assignment. Oops! The door was unlocked, and someone had been in my car! The ignition port was dangling, certainly not ready to receive a key. Someone had tried to steal my car, leaving the evidence of their unsuccessful efforts behind including my car! I had heard the Ford LTD was not easy to steal. Praise God their effort was thwarted! Yes, we were in a rough neighborhood adjacent to the University of Chicago and shared their security system.

There was an interview with the University police and with the Chicago police. Forms needed to be filled out for them and the insurance company involving the next several hours.

When that had quieted down, I started to reflect on my finances. I thought that I could finance my seminary education. I had enough to pay tuition for this year with the severance pay from my nursing position. I took my pension at age 61 (20% reduction) and could squeak by until social security started next year. But now maybe I couldn't make it. I had decided to apply myself to full time study since it had been so long since I had been in school. Having just finished my first quarter, it seemed I had made the right decision.

Well, now I had a car to repair, and I could work as a nurse a day or two a week, evenings, or weekends — many of my classmates were working and University of Chicago Hospital was nearby. Surely, I could do that.

I became quite convinced I would have to supplement my income, so I set about working on a resume for a nursing position. In reviewing my history, I realized it had been fourteen years since I'd worked in a hospital. There would be a lot of stress to make the adjustment to hospital nursing. As I typed the resume, I just couldn't get the columns to line up. This computer was more complex than I had anticipated. I finally gave up and went to bed a bit stressed after a pleading prayer for help.

One of my constant companions for years had been the devotional book, God Calling. As I read the daily reading the next morning, I stopped. And I read it again. The message was, "You can't expect God to give you more until you've used what you have." Well, yes, I had a nest egg in the bank. And I now heard I must use it. I was so relieved! My concern about going to work vanished. Eventually, my car got fixed and paid for. I was led to give my money concerns to God and I did! I was never troubled by financial need again, and I was so well cared for.

In my second year, my LTD Ford didn't pass the CO_2 emission test. I was advised it wasn't feasible to try to have it repaired. I went to talk to the financial aid officer. I was so surprised that he didn't even ask about the small fund I had saved for retirement and gracefully assisted me with what I needed to get a different car. Buying a used car can be troublesome, but a friend taking CPE with me led me to a car dealer near her home in Indiana. He was reliable and trustworthy, and I was happy with my new-to-me used Ford Taurus.

My senior year I applied for a scholarship to assist with tuition. There again, I gracefully was offered and received what I needed. Later I saw a sign on the bulletin board that a parish pastor wanted help in her congregation. It was in an intercity, multicultural church — the one we had been at for Unity and Diversity. I knew of the African American lady pastor, so I answered her notice, not because I needed to make money, but for the experience. I helped with the youth program on Saturday mornings and with worship on Sundays, preaching once a month. I learned so much from the pastor especially about hospitality, outreach in a diverse community, and enthusiasm for ministry. Pastor Washington was a great mentor.

Very helpful was the support money that Grand Rapids Zion congregation sent me occasionally, and the Northeast Minnesota Synod ELCA, my home synod, surprised me with a small check after a synod meeting where they designated part of the offering be divided among their eight seminarians. My needs were met very adequately, and I felt very blessed that I finished seminary without debt. I even had enough cash that I could accompany Zion choir on a mission trip to Germany in July after graduation, but before I was ordained. God knows how to take care of those things if we but trust Her.

CHALLENGES BEGINNING SEMINARY

Seminary was a whole new world for me. I guess I should have understood that I would be using a new language, because for years I'd used a medical dictionary to look up medical terms, but it took some time for me to realize I needed a Dictionary of Theological Terms to understand theology.

I loved to study and to dig into the Bible — to read and think about how different cultures, various groups of people in different times, interpreted those words and how God spoke to the chosen people. The process of opening my mind, my understanding was so phenomenal. I needed to hear about God's love for me and the world, to learn about grace, to accept it for myself. I think I'm still learning.

I began seminary with a five-week course called Unity and Diversity. We were asked to journal daily or often with our reactions, feelings, thoughts about what we had heard and experienced. At the end of the class term our advisor would read our journal. I hesitated to share mine since I'd been journaling for several years and never shared it with anyone. It seemed so personal, between me and God. At the time, it was not clear if I would be going to seminary one year or for a Master of Divinity Degree (MDiv) — a four-year program. My advisor assured me reading my journal would help with discernment on that issue. I agreed to share. This first challenge began to help me open up.

After reading my journal entries, she recommended I begin on the MDiv track. She understood that four years seemed like a long time. There was an alternative route if I felt four years was undoable but she recommended the four-year course. "We women have special challenges in a male dominated profession. A shorter program might accentuate problems that come up," she said. I agreed to try it.

Early on, I learned that my ability to memorize was limited. My first term I studied Greek. I found I could learn the alphabet and about 75 words. I tried and tried to memorize more but they just wouldn't stick! Interestingly, years later when studying Spanish, my vocabulary was well over five hundred words. I never could learn to speak Spanish though; I couldn't hear it or speak it! Apparently a sixty-one-year old brain can expand its capacity.

In the first term I also had difficulty with the Early Church History course. The material was presented chronologically. So much material was covered from 27 AD to 1500 AD. The final test required essays on specific topics like formation of religious organizations and the history of the formulation of the Creeds. We were warned, but I didn't comprehend. I didn't do well (C-). In a similarly constructed course that I took in my senior year, I had learned the method. I received and A. So, it's possible to learn new methods, also.

Yes, I had difficulty learning Greek and Hebrew. But I remember when writing the final exam for Hebrew, an open book exam, the appreciation I experienced in understanding the rich interpretation of the Hebrew text, one that I would have difficulty receiving from a translation. Maybe that's why I frequently have my desk covered with five or so translations when studying the Bible texts. By reading the various translations, I am trying to get a glimpse of the original meaning.

And there were personal challenges. One day I was writing prayers for a simple chapel service. I wanted to pray about how interpretations of certain Scriptures had been harmful to me. All of a sudden, my heart started pounding so fast and so hard I thought I might be having a heart attack! What was happening to me? What caused this change? What could I do? Gradually my heart rate slowed down. I tried to contact my advisor, but she was out of town. Then I turned to the pastor of my parish assignment as I was an associate member there. He was so kind and helpful. He likened my experience to that of Isaiah in Isaiah 6:6-8 where Isaiah was cleansed by the burning coal so that he could speak for God. Pastor explained that I was being given authority to critique interpretations of scripture which I previously did not have. This was the beginning of a process of growing into the role of a pastor. My pastor counselled me to avoid those situations that made me anxious and to proceed only as the Spirit led me with reasonable comfort. I understood that my fast-beating heart was a sign of anxiety as I was moving into new territory, and I now felt confident how I could proceed. This was a memorable God Moment for me.

I CAN'T EVER SEE MYSELF PREACHING

I was in my second year at seminary, taking the Master of Divinity Course which prepares people to become pastors. We were well into the course on Gospels. My assignment was to translate the Gospel lesson from Greek to English and to write about what this gospel lesson said to me.

Sitting at my computer, I was feeling frustrated. My Greek certainly wasn't sufficient to translate anything into English. How could I do this assignment?

I left my computer, walking the two blocks to my professor's office, and he was in. I told him my frustration with not knowing Greek and then I said, "This is preparation for preaching, isn't it?" He agreed that it was. I admitted, "I guess I do have The Interlinear Bible to get the translation, but I can't ever see myself preaching!"

He looked at me kind of strangely and encouragingly said, "Well, just do the best that you can."

I started back to my apartment. As I was walking away, I couldn't believe what I had just said! I realized that I was afraid to preach. I thought back about last Christmas time while driving back to Minneapolis from Chicago. I listened to a sermon by a male preacher on a Christian radio station preaching about the Christmas story. He was so authoritarian, so confident, and calling God, "He." I remember I had thought to myself, I can never preach like that. My training emphasized that God was not masculine. God was a Spirit and gender free. If we forgot, it was circled, and we were reminded to correct it. Yes, it's true that Dr. Grantson, the pastor I heard every Sunday, had a gentle way of sharing the Word as he preached for about thirty minutes and covered all three lessons. I recognized that my sense of authority was weak, and I had some things to work through before I was ready to preach.

I returned to my computer and St. Mark 4:35-41. I'll do the best I can so with my Interlinear Bible. I translated the story about Jesus and the disciples crossing the Lake of Galilee at night. A huge wind storm arose, battering the boat while Jesus was asleep in the stern. The disciples, afraid they were sinking, woke Jesus. "Don't you care that we are sinking?" they said to Jesus. He said, "Peace! Be still!" and the wind ceased. "Why are you afraid? Have you still no faith?" The disciples were filled with great awe saying, "Who then is this, that even the wind and the sea obey him?"

I stopped on that line. **"Who then is this, that even the wind and the sea obey him?"** Suddenly it was like my mind peeled open. A whole flood of ideas flowed past — topics that could be used in a sermon. It was amazing! I sat there, glued to my chair in wonderment. God is alive! God wants me to preach. That's the message I received that day from this scripture.

I have reflected on this scene so many times. I came away with the assurance that God would provide topics and ideas for my sermons. I was reinforced in knowing that the work I had been called to do wasn't all mine; it was a partnership with God. God being the leader. Oh, the privilege of being loved, being honored to be invited to be a partner with God.

One assurance wasn't sufficient here either. I still had doubts. To my delight, for Christmas, I received a book, Weaving the Sermon: Preaching in a Feminist Perspective from Jane, my daughter, by Christine M. Smith which very plainly spoke to my dilemma of finding my voice to preach. Women have a very different experience in life she explained. Their interpretation of the scripture will reflect this, explaining to me that

59

women didn't have to preach like men. I understood from her that I could explore the text from my own perspective. I could raise various possible applications to my daily life. This was very helpful for me.

In the following quarter I was taking a course on Feminist Theology. Carol Gilligan, in her letter to readers, 1993, to her revision of In A Different Voice, clarified some of my background. "Women became aware of the strength of an internal voice which was interfering with their ability to speak. That internalized voice told the woman that it would be 'selfish' to bring her voice into relationships, that perhaps she did not know what she really wanted, or that her experience was not a reliable guide in thinking about what to do. Women often sensed that it was dangerous to say or even to know what they wanted or thought — upsetting to others and therefore carrying with it threat of abandonment or retaliation." I had been raised with this internalized voice that discouraged independent thinking, and anything but submission was reprimanded. With the help of this course and many feminist writers I moved ahead.

IT'S FOR YOU

Some have said that Seminary isn't the appropriate place to go for healing. But Henri Nouwen wrote in the book, The Wounded Healer, that, "in our own woundedness we can become a source of life for others." Many have come for healing and found as that happened, they were prepared for something bigger, to help others in their healing process.

I was aware that in my five years of therapy as an incest survivor, I had not touched my spiritual issues. I puzzled over the realization that our "religious family" that attended church and Sunday School every Sunday, sang in the choir, went to Lutheran Daughters of the Reformation (LDR) and attended Vacation Bible School every summer with my mother as a teacher, could live in a home with constant abuse. We had these good religious teachings, but when we came home, we dealt with lying, secrets, and emotional and sexual abuse. The two didn't match. Where was God, our protector? Where was the loving, forgiving father? Mother? How could I relate to a God called father? When I stood in front of the fireplace and heard the voice of God say, "This (seminary) is for you," I was so astounded, I didn't even hear that God also wanted me to experience God's grace and love. Maybe I didn't even know what that was. But I journaled it. And in seminary I did experience God's grace in so many ways and learned about love which contributed so much to my continued healing. I'll tell of just a few of my God moments.

In my first term, one of my classes was studying the Pentateuch, the first five books of the Old Testament. One of the assignments was to read a book from an assigned list and write a book report on it. I read Texts of Terror: Literary-Feminist Readings of Biblical Narratives by Phyllis Trible. She did a feminist interpretation of five narratives in which women in the Old Testament were treated horribly.

These stories were not unknown to me as I had read through the Bible, and they had made me shudder. But reading this book helped me see that women have been treated in shocking ways as meat, as property, as the object of cunning planning to fulfill man's lust, as the weaker gender who have been dominated with power all through the ages and still are today. The story of Amnon and his sister, Tamar, had a special message for me. My mother repeatedly told me that, disregarding the abuse from my father of my sisters and me, he loved us. Amnon didn't love his sister! He lusted her! After he acted on his crafty plan to rape her, he hated her. He kicked her out of his tent and sent her away frightened and disgraced. I realized that my father didn't love us; he lusted us — constantly. How could that be considered love? I was raised with a false teaching of love. Yes, God, I had something to learn about love and grace.

One comment that lingered with me from the interview that I had with my synod committee when considering seminary was that I was immature. This was said to me after I had shared with them that I had taken a modern dance class and had so enjoyed the freedom of movement. One of the pastors replied that, yes, his daughter, when she was about six took dancing lessons and that had been her reaction. They were judging me immature like a six-year old. I was so devastated.

I did a lot of work on my past abuse in seminary. Every chance I had I would study with female professors. Feminist Theology was a great help to me and when a course on it was offered by my advisor, I took it. I took several other courses at neighboring seminaries, one on images of God taught by a feminist in summer school and another on abuse. It was while I was reading Abuse of Power by theologian, psychoanalyst James Poling that I learned about the disorienting aspect of incest therapy on the personality. The pain and angst raised with repressed memories being

62

uprooted and coming forward caused disruption of the self-concept, he explained, and requires reintegration of the personality. So maybe I was immature. Maybe I had a good reason for it. What a relief it was for me to read his analysis of healing for abused people! A God Moment for me.

Then there was the day when I became so upset, so angry at hearing again how women had been abused. I don't even remember the initiating cause. I remember coming into my apartment so passionately angry. I cried and cried, and I called out to God, "How long, Oh Lord! How long will you allow this abuse of women to continue. It's been going on since the beginning of time, and it's still going on today."

I heard this voice answer me, "That's why I have you!"

In my despair I answered, "Don't give me that. What can I do with it?"

I had an appointment to meet with my advisor shortly thereafter. I went with red eyes, still upset. She understood abuse. She had a rocking chair in her office. She took me on her lap and rocked me, held me, soothed me. What a God moment! Oh, the acceptance, the love, the tenderness, the grace. And after we had talked for some time, she recommended a book, Gyn/Ecology by Mary Daly. She explained that it was a book of rage, of anger. Mary Daly is a brilliant feminist theologian who had been treated unfavorably by the patriarchal church and wrote about her reaction to this sexism, by God, by men, in the Bible, and in the church. She was so angry she could no longer be a Christian. As I was told, it was not an easy read, but it addressed my anger and soothed my spirit as well as giving me many laughs as she deconstructed/reconstructed words in the seven to eight hundred pages. Her anti-Christian themes did not affect my own convictions. God never did give me the opportunity to work in this area, although I was willing and tried to engage at several points.

"An Invitation to Abuse Survivors" was a notice that appeared on the bulletin board at LSTC. A University of Chicago student counselor was requesting participants for a group she was going to start for support to abuse survivors. I called her and thought this would be healthy and helpful. I was willing to try it. I went to the first meeting. Something was not right. She ignored my contributions, wouldn't make eye contact. "What's going on?" I asked, after the meeting.

"You remind me of my perpetrator, my mother," she told me. Whew! She had some healing to do as some counselors do. This was not healthy or helpful. It's a horrible feeling to be in the role of perpetrator. I didn't want to be a part of that, and I wasn't.

The last example on this topic occurred in my New Testament Interpretation course. It was team taught by our two male theologians with fifty to sixty students in the class. First Peter was the New Testament book we used to study the various aspects of the New Testament study and one of the basic courses for preaching. When the class came to the discussion of abuse in chapter two, there was great concern about abuse. It seemed every one of the students could identify someone they were close to who had been abused — mother, sister, girlfriend, grandmother, self. This discussion seemed so unexpected by the professors, and they had to step back and adjust their teaching plan to find a way to deal with this flood of unease. They called in my advisor to help them. It was a little ray of light, of open recognition of the prevalence of abuse influencing our society, especially women, breaking through at our seminary that I was blessed to observe as well as be a part of.

GOD MOMENTS AT CPE

I did my Clinical Pastoral Education (CPE) unit at Christ Hospital in Chicago my second year of seminary.

One day I was asked by the nursing staff to see John, a man diagnosed with a chronic debilitating lung disease. John was hospitalized because his wife was having severe heart problems and was unable to care for him in their home. I was told he was very upset about his condition. I went to see him. John was sitting in bed with oxygen by nasal cannula. He frowned as I entered and introduced myself. He attempted to answer but produced only a gasp for air. I explained that I was a chaplain. I was requested by the nurse to stop by and see him. I understood his difficulty breathing and would do all the talking, as much as possible. He could just listen.

I asked John if my information was correct as I shared that he had been suffering with a lung condition that wasn't expected to improve. "This must be a very frustrating situation," and he nodded in agreement.

Sometimes we can find some help in past situations. Have you had any experience with a higher power? Or ever had anything happen to you that you would attribute to God? Or maybe something has occurred to you that gave you courage or helped you cope when you were in a hard spot?

His face lit up! With his limited respiratory capacity, he told me that when he was in the army — the night before he was to ship out to Europe for D-Day, he had gone to chapel service. As he was walking back to the barracks, it was like a bright light shined on him. It seemed so powerful — it relaxed him. He felt warmth and fullness in his being like never before. John felt this was God promising to protect him. His fear and dread of war left him. He said he came back to the states alive and whole. John always knew God had protected him.

I assured him this power, this God, was still there for him. He relaxed back in his bed, looking so peaceful. I asked if we could pray together. He nodded. Following that, I left the room with him dozing.

Two days later I stopped by his room. He looked relaxed and smiling but not interested in talking. Plans were being made for his discharge to a care center. I really wanted to hear from him how he was but I had to be satisfied with what I saw. That God-Moment a couple of days ago was a connection for him as well as for me.

Another time when I was walking down the hall, I saw an elderly woman patient, lying in bed, pulling at her restraints. The side rails on her bed were up, she was restlessly moving about and moaning. I went in to talk with her. Realizing that she was semi-conscious and unable to respond, I introduced myself, explaining that she was in the hospital, that the cords attached to her wrists and ankles were to protect her from falling and hurting herself. She quieted, and I sat down and talked to her for a while. I asked if I could pray for her. She lay quietly. I prayed, holding her hand, and sang the song, "Jesus Loves Me." I quietly left with her resting peacefully.

I wrote this visit up as a reflection paper and discussed it with my supervisor. In my reflection, I noted that she had reminded me of my mother in her dying process. And as I was reading it tears welled in my eyes and down my cheeks. And my supervisor shed a few tears, also, telling me that it also reminded him of his mother. What a wonderful feeling of grace and understanding to have someone cry with you! It was a special God-Moment.

I became a Grandma for the first time in March. I arrived ten days later after quarter finals. I journaled, 'What bliss it is to hold Daniel close, to nuzzle my cheek against his head, to stroke his blond hair, pat his bottom, hear his grunts and groans. He's such a laid-back child but the softness, the helplessness, the beauty. Become as a little child, Jesus said. Praise you God! What a lesson." A God Moment!

AFRAID OF WHAT?

"Do you have a suggestion for my Internship project?" I asked Leif, my internship supervisor.

"I think with your background, a health project would be good," he said.

"That would be interesting," I answered. "I've had some experience in my home congregation, planning a healing service. Do you have any suggestions for what you'd like included?"

"Why don't we think about it for a week or two and then talk about it?" was his answer.

I was learning about the history of Grace Lutheran Church, where I was doing my internship. The congregation was formed by a group previously members of Zion Lutheran. About twenty years earlier when the charismatic winds were blowing over the mainline Christian churches, the pastor at Grace became involved. He introduced these concepts especially to the youth. He would gather them in the narthex before the service and encourage their support for his teachings. He began advocating for blessing the babies rather than baptizing them, causing rifts in families and against Lutheran theology. Some families actually split up, causing much pain, I was told. My supervisor thought there were still hurt feelings resulting for this and hoped the healing project would help.

In the planning we decided to have a group of congregation members assist with the planning. We decided to begin by offering a class to the congregation studying the Biblical accounts of Jesus' healings. We looked at who sought the healings and how the healings were accomplished. What does the Bible say about healing? About the cause of disabilities like blindness?

We had a health fair, inviting in health agencies to take blood pressures, cholesterol levels, blood sugars. Individual education was offered with handouts. Information was given on the importance of exercise, regular health checkups, weight control, good nutrition.

A junior-high school teacher and I taught a class on drug prevention to the sixth to eighth grade students using Lectio Divina Bible study method on the scripture with them. In Lectio Divina the same scripture passage is read three times. After the first reading the individuals silently, for a minute, reflect on what the passage is saying to her. That is shared with the group in one or two words. Then the passage is read a second time. Now each person spends a minute to think about what those words mean to him/her, sharing their insight. After a third reading, and quiet reflection, each person offers a brief prayer asking for God's help to enable him to use this new understanding. I was amazed that since the Spirit speaks to each of us differently, they identified every point that I would have wanted to highlight in those passages, had I been lecturing. What an effective way to study Scriptures with the young, I thought.

The culmination of the project was a Sunday morning healing service. In planning the service, I called the leader of the prayer chain asking them to pray for the Holy Spirit's presence. This group had been formed earlier in the year. Several days later I had a call back saying some of the people just couldn't pray for the Holy Spirit. They said they were afraid of the Holy Spirit. My first reaction was, "They're afraid of What? Afraid of the Holy Spirit? "After a moment, I recognized why. They had been involved in the events earlier in their history. Of course, they might be afraid — afraid that something like that could happen again. Again pain, families injured. I quickly said, "Well, ask if they could just talk to God about their fear, that they couldn't pray for the Holy Spirit. God understands our fears." I didn't know who was afraid and didn't follow up on this which probably would have been a good thing to do.

The sermon for the healing service included a testimony of a woman whose husband's heart had stopped three times during his surgery. The medical team were calling it a miracle that he was alive. I had had prayer and communion with them the evening before and our staff and others were supporting them in prayer that day. She told of the doctor coming out to her telling her of his complications and his miraculous recovery.

As I encouraged the congregation to come forward for a healing prayer and anointing with oil, I explained that we are all broken, all in need of healing. The pastor and I prayed for each other, anointing with oil. The congregational participation and response was very positive.

The program was planned with continuation in mind and the committee promised to honor that. What a God moment to experience the healing power of the Holy Spirit and also for that experience with the young people in being directed by God's Word!

Sometime later I received a Christmas card from a couple who were trying to start a family. It didn't happen with the healing service, she told me, but they had recently had twins with in-vitro fertilization. She thanked me for the encouragement they received from the healing service.

My internship experience was filled with grace. I was nervous about leading the liturgy and service. Pastor Leif explained to me that the liturgy was the work of the people. If one made a mistake, people would notice it for a few minutes and then forget it. "You don't have to be perfect. If you do the liturgy perfectly, it will be the first time, and it will never happen again," he said.

This helped me relax. This attitude of grace helped me grow in confidence and permeated my internship experience.

SENIOR YEAR AT SEMINARY

My second grandchild, Lucas, a bouncing boy, was born August 29, 1994 to Peggy and Paul, my son. I returned to seminary a week early so I had a chance to get acquainted with him before classes began. When Peggy returned to work in November, I was his babysitter each Friday. We didn't always read children's books. I read Theology — the work of the Holy Spirit to him. And he would look interested. Peggy scheduled his immunizations on Thursdays, so we had days when he was feverish and feeling out of sorts and we would spend much of the day in the rocking chair. I was so blessed, being able to spend that time with him.

Senior year at the seminary was busy. First on the agenda was completing my Application for Candidacy for Ordination. We were given five questions to answer on topics like my gifts for ministry, my personal theology, my ability to preach, etc. I ended with a forty-page paper. This would be considered by my synod committee along with internship, CPE, and seminary reports to determine if I was an appropriate candidate for ordination. My papers were finished by October first and sent off to the committee. We were hoping for an individual conference at the Synod retreat for seminarians later in October.

My candidacy meeting was held from 9:30-11 PM on the first night of the retreat. I was excited and wide awake in spite of starting the day at 4 AM to catch a 6AM flight from Chicago to Minneapolis where I met a ride to the camp. I was thrilled to see my seminary advisor there at my meeting. She had moved to Northern Minnesota the year before and was now on the Candidacy Committee. Also, present was a woman pastor who I met with before I began seminary. She had told me then not to go into ministry if I could do anything else. One of my God Moments here was that I realized that I did have a choice. I'm sure I could have done something else but I chose to go into ministry, to be a pastor. Somehow having a choice seemed very important for me. I am blessed that God allows me to choose! My committee approved my application to be eligible for ordination. The final step in this process, besides finishing seminary, was to be chosen by a congregation to be their pastor.

That fall I noticed a sign on the bulletin board that Pastor Maxine Washington wanted someone to help with her children's program on Saturday mornings. I had heard Pastor Washington, an African American, preach at chapel service. She was a dynamic preacher and someone I would like to know. I applied and was accepted. Her congregation, Spirit of Joy, was a mixed culture Lutheran church, African American and Hispanic, located in a depressed area of Chicago. I worked with an able volunteer and the pastor on a Saturday school for neighborhood children and also helped with Sunday services, preaching once a month. The Saturday school had Bible teaching, singing and fun activities. One day I was visiting an elderly woman who was a shut-in. I was reporting that she needed help to clean her apartment. Pastor Washington told me, that's what you did as a nurse, you're a pastor now and need to focus on her spiritual needs. I needed that reminder. She was a joy to work with.

Christmas was special because my daughters came to Chicago to spend the holiday with Paul and Peggy and me. What a wonderful time we had — two babies. Luke was just three months old and scheduled to be the infant Jesus in his church pageant. Unfortunately, he got strep throat and had to cancel that one. Daniel was twenty-one months and very active. I have a picture of his mother retrieving him from the window sill behind the Christmas tree where he held his portable microphone. We ruined his debut. But he continued standing in front of the fireplace talking (babbling) into a toy microphone like a master of ceremony or maybe a preacher! We were happy to celebrate with Jane and Peter on expecting their first child in May. We ended up having Christmas dinner at Paul and Peggy's, so Luke wouldn't have to go out. What a wonderful family I have!

In March our class in cultural awareness took a trip to South Dakota to the Native American reservations. There we heard about their struggles for identity and self-esteem, and the injuries they suffered from broken treaties by us, our government. One Native American man that talked to us had been going to a Lutheran seminary for a Master of Theology degree and had interrupted those studies because he was drawn back to his native religion. I couldn't imagine how confusing that was for him.

They invited us to their sacred ceremony, their Sweat Lodge. I'm sure we had some orientation to this being an experience of being uncomfortable, a time to accompany our Native American friends in their suffering. They do it for cleansing and to suffer vicariously with those in difficult situations around the world.

We entered this unlit, dark hut seated very closely on the ground in circles. There were ten from our group and another ten Native Americans in a space about the size of a four-man tent. Their leader hung two eagle talons at the door. Then their traditional five stones which had been heated to the extreme in a fire outside were brought in and the door was closed. At first the heat felt good. The hut was pitch black. There was some movement of passing some sage and other herbs around. Some were put on the hot stones and the air, now hot, was scented. My nose began to burn, my throat was dry and became uncomfortable. I tried to relax and join in their prayers. I'm not sure the prayers were in English or what their focus, but I knew you didn't have to understand to pray with them. I tried to keep my thoughts centered on God and their concerns. By now my breathing was becoming a little difficult. They brought in more hot stones. We had a whiff of cool air and daylight. And with the door closed, there were more prayers and silence. Eventually they gave attention to their sacred prayer pipe, the Chanupa. By now I was wishing for a chance to exit the tent as I was getting shaky with difficult breathing. As they finished, I crawled out of the tent, had some water and sat on the grass for some time to recover. It was and honor to have been invited to share that sacred time with them. I had a unique prayer experience and recovered with renewed vigor.

The next day we traveled west to the site of the Wounded Knee Massacre, which occurred in December 1890. This was very emotional for me. How could our army, our country be so cruel to Native Americans? It reminded me of my visit to the cite of the atomic bomb museum and surroundings in Hiroshima, Japan in 1988. Oh, the suffering! The loss of life — the ravages of war. This God Moment touched my heart with sadness and shame for my country. I am so thankful for the promise of God's forgiveness. Consider if you have ever felt the need for forgiveness for something others in power have done?

NOT THE USUAL CALL PROCESS

It was time to look for a job after four years of schooling. The church's procedure for a new graduate of seminary continued with the bishops assigning the approved candidates to one of the nine church's regions. We seniors all waited eagerly for our regional assignment.

The list was posted on April first. I scanned the list for my name — it wasn't there! I asked the seminary coordinator — she checked with the church office. They had no papers for me. I wasn't listed as an approved candidate. What a blow! Upon further investigation, they found my papers in a wrong file. They came in early and were misplaced. The bishops were meeting, and they could assign me then, I was told. That meeting of the bishops in California was devastatingly drenched with heavy rain, and they didn't get to assigning me to a region, so I would be assigned to my original synod, Northeastern Minnesota Synod. Bishop Munson there said he had five candidates. They didn't really need me, but of course he'd try to find a place for me.

I had been in contact with Rev. Cooper-White in the Evangelical Lutheran Church of America (ELCA) office about the papers and now this situation. He told me that California Southwest Synod could use me. He suggested I call Bishop Munson for permission to contact California SW Synod about their need. Bishop Munson gave that permission. My call to California SW was warmly received. Because I was sixty-four years old, it was thought I was not a highly desired candidate for a church. In describing myself I said, "Everyone wants a young pastor — I've been described as someone about thirty years old. They want someone who has had years of pastoral experience. Well, I've had years of experience — just not as a pastor. And they want someone who will stay a long time. I said,

"That's in God's hands." My interest in multicultural ministry was helpful. They asked for my candidacy papers which I sent. Two weeks later I had a phone call from that bishop's assistant saying she had several small congregations that needed a pastor. She would be presenting my papers to one of them. I heard back from her within a week that Epiphany Lutheran in Canoga Park was interested! I flew to Los Angeles to be interviewed on Saturday, April 29, 1995 and preaching there on Sunday.

I was auditing a Bible Course on Revelation that quarter at Seminary. One of the preaching texts for that Sunday, April 30, was Revelation 7: 9-17, about heaven. I remember I said it was like there was a "glass ceiling" between heaven and us. In heaven there are gathered people from every tribe and nation singing their praises to God continuously. Here on earth we are still struggling with sin, with supporting our families, with keeping our faith alive amidst all the things that come up every day. How important it is that we join with the angels and the throngs in heaven worshipping on Sundays adding our thanks and praise to God with those of the saints in heaven. And we can work together here to find ways to share this wonderful hope of ours with those in our community. We look forward to that day when God will wipe away our every tear, when there will be no more hunger or thirst, when we will live with Jesus.

The interview the day before was challenging. They had about fifty members worshipping. The former pastor needed to get a part time teaching position because they couldn't pay him sufficient salary to live on. It seemed like most of the committee felt they had tried everything and had gained very few members. They had six to eight children in the membership which was predominantly elderly. I knew God would guide me to know if this was the right place for me.

Later that day, I visited with Arline and Bernie, friends I knew from Minnesota years before. They were happy to see me They were the only people I knew in that area and they lived twenty miles away. I was excited and felt God so close to me.

Those were busy days. My granddaughter, Laura, was born on May 13. I went to spend several days with her and daughter, Jane, and new daddy, Peter. As I thought about Epiphany, I felt the Holy Spirit call me there.

On Pentecost Sunday, June 4th, I received a phone call telling me that the congregation had voted to call me as their pastor. This was also the day I graduated from seminary. What a celebration! Filled with the Holy Spirit of Pentecost, I felt like I was flying on a cloud. I had a call, a necessity before I could be ordained. Probably the first one in my class. The usual procedure through the regional method took months if not a year. California! A long distance away but I was ready for it now.

MINISTRY AT FIRST CALL
SECTION III

CALIFORNIA HERE I COME — ALMOST

On August 13, 1995 I was ordained at Zion Lutheran Church in Grand Rapids, MN. My ordination invitation read: "When the fullness of time came, God called Margie to ordained ministry."

Participants included: The Reverend Doctor Nancy Hess as Presider, the Reverend Doctor Maxine Washington as preacher, and Bishop Paul Egertson, Bishop of SW California Synod, ordainer. I was blessed to have several people from my internship congregation in Muscatine, Iowa present. My friend, and seminary classmate, Timothy Dean led the prayers, and my friend, Gerri Licke presented me for ordination. Pastor Eiesle of Zion was the host, and Zion's choir (of which I was a member for many years) honored me with their music. I was blessed as I took my vows to serve God and the church faithfully and received the blessing of laying-on-of-hands by the Bishop and clergy. I was surrounded by the same host of family and friends who would support me in my ministry. It was a beautiful day!

The next day in Minneapolis, I had the privilege of going briefly to the ELCA Triennial Church Gathering — celebrating the twenty-fifth anniversary of the ordination of women in the ELCA. I had heard many stories of the blessings that women pastors brought to the Church. I'd also heard of their experiences of being rejected by congregations, and by individual men and women congregants. I am so thankful to each one of the women for their part in preparing the way for me. The gender issue was still alive then, and it is now, but much work had been done.

Gerri, my friend, accompanied me on the road trip from Minneapolis to California. It took us four days to arrive in Sacramento where her son was living.

During that time, I recalled how quickly my summer had passed. I joined Zion's choir on tour to Germany through "Luther Land," the places where Martin Luther, the founder of the Lutheran church, lived and worked. And how fun it was to travel with this group. My sister, Georgia, traveled with me as well as the other fifty-eight including my good friends, Alice, Dee, and Wanda, Pastor and Mimi Eiesle, and choir people who I had known for years.

Luther, a Catholic priest, wanted reform in the Catholic Church, but was expelled for speaking out. His life was threatened, and he hid out in Wartburg Castle. It was a God Moment to see the room where he spent months translating the Bible into the German language. There he experienced the devil so vividly he threw his bottle of ink at it, leaving a splash mark on the wall.

The concentration camp at Auschwitz was also an emotional visit. The millions of people who were murdered there – so impossible to fathom. Help us Lord, to make sure that type of atrocity never happens again! Not a happy God Moment.

But another God Moment happened when Georgia and I got separated from the group. We were weaving through a crowed street going, I'm not sure where. That was probably the problem! But we found ourselves in a beautifully quiet prayer room honoring Saint Elizabeth of Hungary.

Living in the early thirteenth century, Saint Elizabeth was a princess, a queen and a mother who became a widow and was exiled by her in-laws. Destitute, she remained firm in her faith, caring for her three children and serving the poor. We had a quiet interlude there amongst a busy day of sight-seeing.

Following the tour, I stayed five days, going to Hungary to visit a seminary friend. From the beautifully wood carved, stained glass decorated Lutheran churches in Germany I went to the simple, plain Reformed churches in which my friend, Eva was a pastor. It was so wonderful visiting Eva, seeing her in her own environment. She was experiencing difficulty in getting a pastoral assignment, feeling discrimination as a woman. We did local sightseeing as well as going into Budapest to visit her mother. I also had the privilege of visiting a town well known as a tourist center for its mineral water springs hosted by a young lady that I met on the train.

Back in Hopkins where my daughter Jane lived, I had the special privilege of baptizing Laura, my third grandchild at her church in July. And there was time to play with the grandchildren in the Minneapolis area and celebrate my oldest sister Arline and Conrad's fiftieth wedding anniversary.

I took another trip to Los Angeles to find housing. Future parishioners, Bea, accompanied by Betty, drove us around looking at various apartments. The 6.4 earthquake was just eighteen months earlier and a number of apartment buildings were being retro-fitted and repaired. I remember the last one we looked at — it was also being repaired. Betty went with me and Bea, waited in the car. I found a nice apartment and decided to take it. I said, "It's too bad you didn't get to see it, Bea, instead of sitting in the car."

She replied, "I wasn't just sitting here. I was praying." I was so happy to hear that! People who pray are dear to my heart!

Threaded throughout the summer was making preparations for the ordination. The participants were invited, invitations were prepared and sent, the secretary at Zion Lutheran prepared the bulletin and my friend, Wanda, arranged the reception.

One final task was to return to Chicago to see my belongings packed up and on the truck to California and clean out the apartment. Then my ordination and now I was on the road.

There was ample time for conversation, and Gerri and I have never had a problem with that. One topic I remember talking about was our favorite mode of transportation. I said mine was the canoe. I liked the way it glided through the water so quietly, making very small waves in contrast to the speed boats that are noisy and leave other boats in their wake. Then we talked about birds or animals we identified with. Gerri said she liked the owl. She liked to be a mentor and thought of herself as a wise owl. She was a psychiatric nurse, and I could see that! My preference was the peacock. I liked the beautiful colors when it spread its tail. It reminded me of how I felt about my life. How it opened up these last years: how gracious God has been to me.

We kept our bird images alive by gifting each other with their favorite. Gerri was more successful than I in finding variety.

What bird or animal would you identify with and why?

FINDING OUR WAY

What are the possibilities? I came to a small congregation with about one hundred twenty members, fifty at worship, on a good day. Five children were of Sunday School age. The apartments across the street housed Hispanic families who identified with the Catholic religion. Nearby family homes were enclaves of mostly Asians of various origins.

I knew I needed to start slow. We began with small group "get acquainted with the new pastor" meetings held in members' homes. I asked each of them to tell me their dreams for their congregation — what did they like and what would they like different. I heard that many were happy with their "family group," the fellowship that they had. I heard that they had been trying for years to reach out to the community. They tried adding a Hispanic ministry with some funding from the larger church. The funds ran out and the project disappeared. Their last full-time pastor had to get a part-time job because he couldn't live on the salary the congregation was able to pay. Several expressed concern that we might grow too large – too fast! Another concern was voiced, "They always say we have to change. Why can't 'they' come in and be like us?" I asked, "What do you think we could do in our community?" And I heard, "I think we have tried everything."

I was at Epiphany for four and a half years. We had regular worship each Sunday with Sunday School for the five children. We celebrated church holidays, birthdays, had choir concerts, and potlucks. The women made quilts which they donated to the hospital or other organizations.

Early on, there was a need expressed by the nearby elementary school for an after-school program. We were trying to figure out how we could do that when the Boys and Girls Club came in and met that need.

The School District used our building to teach English as a Second Language (ESL) three times a week. Various AA and chemical dependency groups met in the evenings. A lovely lady, Sylvia, came by wanting to begin a class for Hispanic women, teaching nursing assistance. It would meet in conjunction with the ESL class. She called her program BASE, which I recall represented Basic Adult Spanish Education.

Many of her students had no previous education, so it was a real struggle for them. But what a gift to the community! Completion of the class would make them employable. There was little income from these various programs, and congregational finances were a concern.

And then, surprise! I received a letter from Pastor Ede, the same pastor who had been my Confirmation class instructor fifty years earlier. He sent me $1,000 saying he thought that I might need the money for my retirement — or I could use it for ministry. I chose to use it for ministry.

Pastor Ede was in Morris, MN and helped out at our family's home church when we were without a pastor. My sister, Jeanette had met him in Minneapolis in 1994. I had connected with him and then had invited him to my ordination. He was unable to participate — he was still preaching at age 90. What a blessing he was!

While looking for an outreach project for Epiphany, we became aware of a need by the Los Angeles Police Department for assistance with a Drug & Gang Prevention program – Project Amigos. They needed treats to be served after their weekly program for kids — playing ball or some other outdoor activity. We would purchase and distribute the treats and could add other activities if we wanted. Members Virgil and Marty offered to purchase the treats. I was there to distribute them and often added another activity. Sometimes another volunteer would help. Our older parishioners had difficulty helping. The space we used had no sound softeners and

84

thirty to forty kids were extremely noisy. We worked with Project Amigos for several years. Marty and Virgil were wonderful helpers and very reliable. This was a very worthwhile community project.

In 1998, Pastor Ede sent me money again — this time $500. With the council's approval, it was used to hire a childcare giver for mothers who were taking a childcare class given by BASE. How valuable that was for the women. They were learning to care for their own children and getting experience caring for the children of their classmates, under supervision. At the completion, they would be certified to work in a childcare setting.

I visited Pastor Ede several times when I was in Minneapolis to see my family. He shared with me that the prosecuting attorney involved in my father's sentencing to prison was a member of his congregation. The attorney had been so upset by the case that he had come to talk to his pastor. Pastor Ede remembered me as a member of that class of confirmands. He urged me to help others with similar trauma.

How we appreciated his monetary gifts at Epiphany. They enabled us to do effective ministry in our community, and it helped the congregation feel involved in ministry.

We tried an outdoor service with guitar and keyboard for a short time, with no community response. We advertised for a guitarist and hired Ty Longlyn. I know little about him, except he was a very good guitarist and a very pleasant young man. Our experiment lasted only two months. Soon after, we heard that Ty (age 32) was killed in a Rhode Island nightclub fire where his well-known Rock band "Great White" was playing. I was disappointed with the outcome of the outdoor services, but do you think maybe they were meant to be for Ty? I am happy he had that experience with the Gospel.

We had a lovely group of people, but they were comfortable and content. If you asked them to invite a friend, their friends were in the church. They worked to keep up normal routines. Maude tended the rose garden; Betty prepared communion every Sunday; Bea and Barbara kept the quilting group going. The men struggled to keep the cooling system going and the building and grounds in order. Ten to twelve people sang in the choir. It was the same group, plus some I have forgotten to mention worked. We did help another congregation, Nkuhngu Lutheran Church in Dodoma, Tanzania as they built their church. We had a Mission Sunday each year for 3 years and sent about $500 each time. It did not seem like much, but oh, they really appreciated it.

As Epiphany was gradually losing energy and finances, we began talks of merging with a neighboring Lutheran congregation.

I'M HERE FOR YOU

When I came to Epiphany Lutheran Church, I was told by some of the members that they didn't think I should get too close to them. Their early pastor had become one of them, they said, and lost his perspective as a pastor. This made me wonder where I would find support.

A few months after I came, the council decided to have a workshop. Their topic was "Using Your Gifts." They identified a lady who was a motivational speaker to be the presenter. I called her, and she said she would love to come. Lynda Jean gave a good presentation. She stayed afterwards, and talking to me she said, "I did the presentation, but I really came for you". She knew the previous pastor and felt I would need some support. I was really surprised that she would come befriending me — a God Moment.

She was a wonderful friend. She invited me into a group of women friends. We met sometimes monthly — celebrating birthdays, sometimes holidays. We were different religions and various ages. They opened my eyes to many new concepts of life and religion — California style.

Someone invited me to a professional women's book club in Thousand Oaks with several of the professors at California Lutheran College. I thoroughly enjoyed the book discussions we had. A number of the books we read were on woman's issues, which helped me keep that interest alive. It was very stimulating to be a part of, or to just listen to the discussion. I met a woman here who later became my spiritual director. A lovely lady to know.

I had a supportive ministerium, consisting of the local Lutheran Pastors. In addition, San Fernando Valley had many Lutheran churches. The valley was settled mostly in the 1950s when the space program was developing. Many engineers and their families came from the Midwest, many of them Lutheran. There were many Lutheran denominations at that time that had been formed within specific immigrant heritages. Augustania Lutherans had Swedish, Finnish, German, Lutheran Free, etc. Each group had their own church or two in the valley. I was told when the pastor came to establish a United Lutheran congregation, the housing developments would be filled very quickly after they were built. The pastor would go house to house, introducing himself, and inviting the people to join him. When he finished canvassing one development, another would be ready to be visited. The name "Epiphany" was chosen for the congregation that was established — which meant a sudden happening.

When I arrived years later, the families had grown, and the children had moved elsewhere. As I walked around the neighborhood, the Chinese would be in one area, Taiwanese in another, Hispanic in another, etc. The population of the valley had changed. The Lutheran church had changed also. In 1988, there was a major merger within Lutheran denominations, resulting in the Evangelical Lutheran Church of America (ELCA). Many of the Valley churches were under this new umbrella synod. This resulted in three other ELCA churches being within a mile of Epiphany, two of them small congregations, and struggling to survive. We pastors supported one another, becoming a strong support group. We also had help from the area Bishop and his staff.

Two of the women pastors were especially supportive of me. Pastor Ann befriended me and helped with my installation service, and it was through her influence that I became involved in community action. She left for the East Coast about a year after I arrived. Pastor Synde, also, became a good friend and mentor to me. Along with my spiritual director, I felt well supported.

OBSTACLES TO BLOOMING WHERE YOU ARE PLANTED

Dealing with the homeless gave me a few "God Moments." Our church, located on a busy state highway, Topanga Canyon Avenue, was quite isolated. The parking lot, marked off for a basketball court, was by the street. The church sanctuary was facing the parking lot with the social hall and meeting rooms behind it. Attached in the back was the church office facing the parking lot and the pastor's office on the back side. In California style, the rooms were not connected internally. All had outside doors.

We had apartment buildings across the street. To the left was Green Thumb Nursery, a large, busy nursery. They also had the lot on the right side of the church for growing plants, and they rented the back of our church lot to store potted trees. The isolation made it an attractive place for some of the many homeless people who were around the area.

Barbara, a long-time member of our congregation, was the church secretary. She worked 9 am to 1 pm. It was a comfort to have another person around since It was such a quiet setting.

One morning when I was working in my office, I became very uncomfortable. It was like a cautious, uneasy feeling that something wasn't right. I went outside and looked around. I didn't see anything unusual. I decided to do a prayer walk around the building, checking the doors as I went. There, in the front of the church behind the bushes was someone's belongings. There was a nice man's bathrobe with a Nordstrom label, a sleeping bag, and suitcase. A man had been sleeping here. There was a tinge of fear, a feeling of caution and concern for anyone who had to sleep in the bushes — someone who shopped at Nordstrom's! Later that afternoon he came on his bicycle. He said he had separated from his wife and couldn't afford a hotel. I didn't have money for lodging but did offer him a coupon for grocery money telling him he couldn't sleep here. He left on his bicycle.

One morning, when Barbara was on vacation, I came to work to find a surprise. As I came around the corner going to my office, a man was lying in his sleeping bag on the sidewalk! I gasped! He acted like nothing was out of the ordinary. I was standing there with my arms full of books telling him this wasn't a place he could sleep. He was so friendly and wanted to talk about women being pastors. I asked him to leave and eventually he did.

Probably the only time I felt fearful was when Roger, with the council's approval, gave a homeless man that had been sleeping in a hammock in the tool shed, permission to continue to sleep there. He was going to "watch over" the property, making sure others did not sleep or hang around there. It wasn't a proper place for anyone to sleep but it wasn't my decision. Things went smoothly for a few weeks. One afternoon when I was working in my office, I heard a loud angry voice. I locked my door and tried to call Roger. Then the man was pounding at my door, yelling, cursing and sounding very irrational. Roger was not available, so I called the police. I had only one door to my office and that was to the outside. Yes, I was safe inside, but I was frightened, and it seemed like a long time until the police came and removed him from the property. Roger saw him later and explained that the man had taken chemicals. He would not be back.

Another day, we found the quilts which our ladies had made laying on the floor in the social hall. They were left there like someone wanted to be noticed. Eventually the same man who had been sleeping in the bushes came back. He said he had found a window unlocked, opened it and had been sleeping inside! The warning went out — lock the windows!

On a warm, summer day, I had an eerie experience. I was painting the office and had kicked off my sandals. When I went into the women's restroom the cement floor felt warm to my bare feet. The restroom floor was warm! The only possible explanation was that someone had been sitting in there recently. It's hard to imagine why someone had been sitting on the floor in the women's restroom in the back of the building while I was painting the office on the other side. That was puzzling. We never found the answer...It made me think that there was more activity around our church building that we were aware of.

One of our neighboring pastors came by one day. Looking around, he asked, "You work here alone? Do you feel safe? It looks so isolated." There were a number of God Protection Moments, but I was never harmed.

Barbara liked to do things the way she always had. Don't we all? I felt I was called to this congregation to make some changes. I thought we should use a computer, change the 9x15 mimeographed newsletter to 81/2 x 11 computer printed newsletter — among other things. Barbara and I got along, but I often felt her resistance. Eight to ten months later I said to her one day, "Barbara, I feel I was called to this congregation to try to help it grow, and I feel you resisting me. I am trying to move ahead, and it seems like you are pulling against me. It's just you and me working here, and I would like to work as a team, working together. How do you see it?" She said she really didn't think that she was pulling against me.

The next day I took her out to lunch. There she told me she wanted to resign. She had been trying to learn to use the computer but said she didn't want to struggle with that. She said she was really doing this for me. When you want to do something differently, that person won't know how it's been done, won't know it's a change, and they won't resist. "I'm almost retirement age, and I think it's time for me to leave."

I was shocked. That was not my intention nor was it my goal. I commended her for her good work, for her faithfulness and dependability.

I am sure that there were God moments that I missed. One was when an adult of the congregation wanted the former pastor, now retired, to baptize their baby. I hesitated to say yes immediately. Before I could get back to them, the baby's father got impatient, and they planned a private service in the grandparent's backyard with the church friends attending. This generated negative feelings toward me. In a private conversation with the grandparents later, the grandfather told me I wasn't suited to be a pastor. The seminary should have screened me out, etc. I knew he was angry with me. I also knew him as someone having very strong opinions and making blunt criticisms, and I could forgive and let it go.

Another was getting irritated instead of taking time to listen and explain. Several times one man asked me how I could be in charge of the service every Sunday. His aunt was a preacher, and she could only preach when someone gave her permission. I would give him a short answer, like "That's what I'm here for." or "This is my job." This really bothered me. Finally, one day I sat down with him, explaining that I went to seminary for four years to prepare to be a pastor. I was approved for this position by the seminary and the church, the ELCA. Then congregation voted to call me to come and be their pastor, and I was hired to be their leader, their preacher. As we talked about it, he realized his aunt was an evangelist. She preached only when she was asked and was not hired to work with the congregation full-time. He was satisfied and never asked me about it again.

I am sure there were other times that I missed, but God forgives and led me on.

THE DECIDING VOTE

Pastor Ann introduced me to involvement in community issues. One issue I became involved with was Los Angeles' discussion about how many people were on minimum wage with no health insurance. At the airport, LAX, all of the concessions and many of the service attendants were contracted out to private venders. In doing so, the workers were hired by the contractors at minimum wage which was around five dollars an hour. Many women, single mothers, were in their group. Without health insurance, they would be on medical assistance. Their families' health costs were coming out of taxes. To cover living costs, often mothers would have to work two jobs, leaving children to care for their siblings. Very little parental time for family.

The organization I volunteered for gathered at LAX one day. I was dressed in my Alb and stole, carrying a sign asking for living wage for the workers. We met with our local council woman and explained our concern. We learned that she held the deciding vote within the council. One day, shortly before the vote, I was in her office building for another matter. She came out of her office just as I entered the hall. I walked over to her and said I wanted to speak with her. She said, "Walk with me down the hall, and we can talk."

I explained how concerned I was regarding the issue of a living wage. I said it was so difficult, especially for single mothers to have enough time to care for their children. Sometimes even needing two jobs. And the children wouldn't receive parenting. I hoped she would vote for a living wage. She told me that what she needed was for me to talk to businessmen for their support on the issue. We arrived at her destination, and I promised I would do that. I did — with one of the businessmen in my congregation.

The next day, when the vote was taken, the councilwoman supported the living wage raising minimum wage to nine dollars an hour with health insurance and $10.50 without.

That was a God Moment for me. It reminded me of being at a prayer vigil on a hillside at a Global Mission Event several years earlier. We were praying for the freedom of Namibia in Africa. Later that year, the world news announced that Namibia gained its freedom from South Africa. I worked on other issues, but this experience stuck in my memory.

Have you ever advocated for any social issue? Remember to ask God to help you.

ANOTHER VIEW OF AFRICA

The invitation arrived. The Gospel Choir of my seminary was asked to come to Tanzania. Bishop Muamasika, who graduated with my class with a Doctorate in Ministry at the Lutheran School of Theology in Chicago (LSTC), had invited the choir to Dodoma, Tanzania in July of 1997. The invitation was to present and past choir members. I had been a member and loved it during the three years I was at the seminary.

It would be a multi-cultural group with some students and some ordained pastors. The group consisted of eight African-Americans, eight Caucasians, two Hispanics, and a Chinese-American. We had an African-American director and the leader of the group was the LSTC registrar who had organized the choir about ten years earlier.

The primary focus of the choir trip was the biennial meeting of the Tanzanian Lutheran Church, Dodoma Diocese – a regional section of the church. We sang for the worship and meetings. We sang with Tanzanian church choirs. The ordained pastors in our group were asked to preach at one of their churches on one Sunday. Their church was just beginning to ordain women, so the Bishop wanted his congregational members to see women pastors.

For me, the highlight of the trip was the multi-cultural aspect. The African-Americans were processing their history of slavery. Their relatives had been captured years earlier and forced into slavery. I remember one group member saying, "My grandparent wasn't a slave. He was free! He was taken by force and treated cruelly by no choice of his own, made a slave."

Our group would meet at 11 P.M. after rising at 6 A.M. Our African-American friends would be wide awake, excited, discussing their feelings

95

and frustrations in heated, emotional conversations. We Caucasians, especially me, could hardly keep our heads up or our eyes open. One Hispanic lady did not have these issues. She was telling of her peoples' hurts from mistreatment by missionaries in South America.

The choir trip certainly was a wonderful, sometimes sad, learning experience. These topics weren't new to me; we had a women's group at seminary where racial injustice was discussed. I also had talked through some of these issues with a classmate and close friend in seminary who was African-American. But this trip was good.

Another God Moment happened in the meeting room. I was honored to be asked to lead devotions for one of the sessions. I prayed for guidance. I noticed that there were nearly an equal number of Tanzanian men and women delegates attending the business sessions. The men sat in the front and did most of the talking. The women held to the back and were mostly quiet. I wanted to find a Scripture reading that would uplift the women. My roommate, Marilyn, and I talked about it. I looked at the story of Mary and Martha in Luke 10, in the Contemporary English Version of the Bible that I had with me. I was surprised and delighted to read in verse 38, "She (Martha) had a sister named Mary who sat down in front of the Lord and was listening to what he (Jesus) said." I used this Luke Scripture to highlight how Jesus affirmed Mary for listening to him. Jesus had affirmed me, calling me into the ministry after years of believing that I was not worthy of his love, of his attention. Jesus had sent me God Moments (well, maybe I didn't call them that then), talking to me, guiding me. God wanted this for all of us. The reading talks of Mary **sitting in front** of Jesus, not at Jesus' feet, as many translations do. We, all of us women, are honored by Jesus. I said, "You are women who were sent here to represent your congregations! Your women!" I encouraged then to speak up, to share their ideas, their concerns. We are all called to do that.

In African-American style, I can hear the "Amens" and the "Preach it Sister" calls from my group, as well as the filling of the Holy Spirit. And I also noticed that at least some of the women moved to the front at the next session.

I was surrounded by God Moments, but I mention just a few. I probably missed many more. We have to be vigilant to recognize them.

We visited quite a number of mission projects. At the end of our stay, we also visited game parks, with all the beautiful animals, giraffes, rhinoceros, zebras, lions, (tigers were tricky to see), and many more. It was beautiful!

It was here that I met Paul Mwanga and his family. I stayed at his mother's home when we were assigned a homestay. Her husband, a government worker, had died several years earlier. She had converted one section of her building to a place to raise chickens. She sold eggs and chickens to support the family.

Paul Mwanga worked for the Lutheran Church and helped plan our trip. He also accompanied our group on our side trips and to northern Tanzania when we visited the mission projects and game parks. I had a number of conversations with him and enjoyed getting acquainted with him. Paul later came to study in the United States for a Master of Theology, and I was able to connect with him again then.

Another connection I made in Tanzania was with Nkuhungu Lutheran congregation. That's where I was assigned to preach. We met in a schoolroom. The band, children's choir, and congregation members were all packed in. The devotions I had mentioned earlier, and this service were my first experiences using an interpreter. Actually, I liked it. After the service, we went to the place where their church building would be built. They had the church foundation outlined with bricks. They showed me how they made their own bricks, using their clay soil with cement mix and water. They needed help with the cement costs. I went home to Epiphany to see if we could help them, and we did!

Has anyone asked you for help?

STRUGGLING TO MOVE ON

After three years I began looking for a new call. Remember when I said my first call, which took only two months wasn't normal? This time, over the next year I sent my application to fifteen synods. I interviewed for pastor positions in Minneapolis, Eastern Washington, Portland, OR and Southern California. The earlier applications had my age, sixty-eight, on the mobility papers. Then later, when asking for birthdate, I would just include the day and month. When one bishop asked me about the year, I told him I thought he just wanted to celebrate my birthday with me (it is an illegal question to ask.) After that interview I told him that I was 69. He thought I was ten years younger.

A year later, I interviewed at a Lutheran care center. The outgoing chaplain encouraged me to come there. I also interviewed at a congregation for a half-time pastoral care position. I would be working with three established volunteer groups; parish nurses, deacons, and friendly visitors. They had recently paid off their church debt and were adding staff. There were two pastors and they were adding a full-time youth worker and a half-time pastoral care position. The senior pastor seemed hierarchical to me. I expressed some hesitation in private conversation with him. He insisted that I identify my issue. I explained that I had heard of female pastors having difficulties in some settings with strong senior pastors. I wanted to avoid such a situation. He strongly assured me that that would never happen here. I heard him, and I wanted to believe him.

I had a choice! I could accept a full- time call to a Lutheran Senior Care center. I had worked primarily with senior citizens for 14 years in public health nursing. I had spent over four years working with a small struggling congregation with mostly elderly people. That made working with an active congregation look very inviting to me. It would be five to six weeks before the congregation would vote. I felt a strong call to serve this congregation.

Sunday morning, December 5, 1999 I received a phone call informing me that the congregation had voted to call me. I offered my resignation that day at Epiphany. I moved from Canoga Park, about two hours south to Poway, California for my new parish assignment on January 6, 2000.

MINISTRY OF PASTORAL CARE
SECTION IV

I HAVE CHOSEN YOU

My first day, a Tuesday morning, at the Pastor's office we had a pastors' meeting; the Senior Pastor, the Associate Pastor and me. The Senior Pastor and the Associate Pastor loved to tell jokes, so we always had a laugh or two. The Senior Pastor would go over his schedule and other information that he had to share. He said he had not gotten around to planning the off-site council retreat which would be held in ten days. It would be my responsibility. I would have a Bible Study Friday night and Saturday and plan and preach at the worship service on Sunday morning. The Senior Pastor and the Associate Pastor would return to the congregation for regular Sunday Services. The retreat was held in the winery district, twenty miles to the North.

Then he told me he would really like me to go to a meeting of ecumenical church leaders at noon that day. I was to bring a bag lunch. It was led by the chaplain at the hospital who he went on to describe at great lengths and wanted me to meet.

It was nearly noon, and my office was just as I had left it Thursday night after unloading the moving truck — boxes one on another. I thought about the lunch meeting - I had no box lunch, we were in a residential area (box lunches not readily available.) I stopped next door at the Pastor's office and told him that I would be happy to go to that meeting - next month- as I had no lunch and I felt the need to unpack my office.

Plan a retreat - for next week. He had told me on the phone that *he* was going to do that. I could do that. I had to unpack my books to find a resource and I started in on my office.

The schedule I was given for my half-time position was Tuesday 9-5, Thurs 12-8:30 PM because of evening meetings, Saturday 10-2, and

Sunday AM for services. I asked the Pastor for one weekend off each month - the last weekend- and he agreed. I asked if I could preach one Sunday per quarter. The Pastor said that he was the preacher and that preaching was not part of *my* call.

I said that I was called to be a pastor here. I felt that to be recognized as a pastor by the congregation, it was important that I preach occasionally. I thought it was a very reasonable request to preach once a quarter. He was not agreeing with me.

On Wednesday the next week, my day off, I drove to see the retreat center where the council retreat would be held. This was a brand-new area for me and I wanted to get a feel for the setting. It was a nice sunny day, so I sat on the deck, reading from the Bible from Luke chapter 9. I was praying for the retreat, about the plans I was making for it, and also about my conversation with the Pastor about preaching. I read on about Jesus with the disciples James, John and Peter. "And a cloud came and overshadowed them... then from the cloud came a voice that said, 'This is my Son, my chosen: listen to him!'." verse 35.

I read it again, it was saying to me, "Margie, you are my daughter, my chosen: listen to her!" I read it again! I felt God speaking to me in the Word, affirming me to preach at that congregation.

I talked to the Pastor the next day and described this experience. He was quiet. And I then heard him agree to let me preach four times a year. He scheduled me several times the first year. The second year it did not happen. It is amazing to have an experience like that! Have you ever heard God speak to you?

The pastoral care at Incarnation was not only done by the pastors but by three groups of volunteers that I was working with. The deacons assisted with Sunday morning worship, took communion to people who couldn't get to church and conducted worship services in Senior Care Centers. The met monthly. These men and women were a select group that were gifted with an overnight retreat each year. Those were special times for group fellowship and study. For one retreat we decided to study Luther's Small Catechism. They chose to each take one commandment and we discovered there were various divisions of the commandments. We ended up with a scramble which was solved when I got copies of Luther's Small Catechism for each of them.

The nurses were a group of about five ambitious women. They held a health fair to educate the congregation on current health practices and the need for Living Wills, Durable Power of Attorney of Health Care and Trusts. Their aim was to confer with each member who was diagnosed with a serious illness or had health concerns. And they did it! Their assistance was appreciated very much.

The third group was the Incarnation Friends who made friendly visits to those who were lonely or homebound. We met together every two months for support and encouragement.

My interest in healing ministry was useful here. Healing services for the whole congregation was held twice a year and was well received. But there was awareness of a need for a weekly prayer service where we encouraged community participation. Each Tuesday morning, I would have a simple healing service with hymns and Bible verses from the devotional Daily Texts. I would give a short meditation, offer individual prayer, and anointing with oil to each participant.

One elderly couple with various health problems came every week. They so appreciated it. The husband died several months after I left. His wife called and asked if I would go along when they scattered his ashes in the bay. She was on the bank waving at us, while we were in the boat in the designated area, scattering his remains with scripture and prayer.

I remember the morning of 9/11/01. I just happened to turn on my television while getting ready for work. I saw the plane crash into one tower and then the other. I had difficulty comprehending what was happening. It looked like fiction to me, but I finally realized the tragedy. Everyone of the staff was upset. We realized the horrible thing that had happened. Staff meeting centered on the tragedy. I invited the other pastors and staff that could to join me at the healing service for prayer. I was so disappointed that none of them came. The Pastor organized a service 10 days later.

Our pianist for the healing service was diagnosed with advanced cancer. How sad. I spent time with her and her husband praying for healing and for relief of guilt for ignoring symptoms. Her cancer didn't get healed but the rift that had developed among her family members was eased. That was a blessing for her and her husband — yes for all of them.

The first few months I was there I was hearing requests for me to teach them to pray. The Pastor seemed surprised but gave me permission to do a survey for interest. With that established I had three sessions in June on prayer. I started with their experience, formal prayer, then introducing walking prayer, bidding prayer and different forms of meditative prayer and a brief introduction to Centering prayer. There was interest in learning more about Centering prayer so after the new year, I scheduled a full day of orientation and a Centering prayer group was formed. Sherlene, my walking friend came to the prayer sessions, continued into centering prayer and today leads the group!

IMPOSSIBLE!

Sherlene was in my office. She had come to the classes on prayer and wanted to get acquainted. She told me she liked to walk. She walked five miles every day. I asked her why and she said she did it just for fun. I said, "You walk five miles every day just for fun?" I couldn't believe it! It reminded me of the one time I had walked home from school, five miles from town to our farm and almost had a heat stroke. I was a high schooler, didn't know anything about needing water or wearing a hat in the hot sun. That experience didn't encourage me to do long distance walking.

Sherlene invited me to walk with her. We walked probably about two miles. She told me that she and a friend had raised money for breast cancer and did a three-day walk in Washington, D.C., a sixty-mile walk. It was a challenge, she said, but she was so happy to have completed it. About this time, I had a niece, Audrey, a lovely, bright fifty-six-year-old mother, nurse professor with her doctorate was diagnosed with liver cancer. She died within a couple of months. Later when Sherlene told me there was going to be a three-day walk in San Diego I was interested. I would do it to honor Audrey.

They called it Impossible! Raise Fifteen hundred dollars in donations for breast cancer and walk sixty miles in three days. One part seemed as impossible as the other. Sherlene was going to do it again. We'd train together. Peggy and Nancy joined us walking. They had completed the walk previously. This time they would be volunteers on the support team. Peggy's husband joined in walking after he recovered from a health issue. And sometimes Dick, Nancy's husband came too.

We went to classes on stretching and how to condition. I got walking shoes, specially fitted. The first pair resulted in blisters, so I tried another

107

and they worked much better. In the middle of the training, I became ill after a session of ministry — an episode of asthma. A test for tuberculosis came back positive which required I stay away from people. I remember the weather was bright and sunny. By now I felt good, so I would walk six to seven miles in the morning and again in the evening. After a week the positive test result was proved an error. I don't have TB after all. But I kept walking. I don't think I ever walked more than nine miles at a time while training but would walk twice a day.

The walk was in the spring of 2002, after nine-eleven 2001. The route for the walk originally was planned to go around the airbase. That area was now was restricted. It was changed to go along the coast, up and down many hills, especially the first day. And there were so many people! They expected five thousand participants and had over six thousand. It was slow going but exhilarating. I can still see the women wearing flip-flops, developing blisters — eventually very serious blistered feet. There were children with their moms — probably for shorter distances. I remember mostly women of all ages (with an occasional man) some being in treatment for cancer, some in wheelchairs, some with survivor t-shirts. Every so often there would be snack tables and port-a-potties with long lines. Lunch would be served from the snack tables around noon. We'd sit on the grass. After eating we'd take off our shoes and massage our feet. I got by with mild leg cramps, relieved by Tums, and two small blisters which responded to first aid.

And we made it. They had tents for us to sleep in — we were camping! and a food tent for breakfast and dinner. We didn't need much entertainment. Rest, caring for our feet and achy muscles and even a blister or two was what I needed.

And I raised not $1,500 but $2,414! So surprising especially since I have never been a great supporter of events like this. How thankful I was to all those who had contributed! With prayers for the money collected for successful research and support for clinics for cancer detection.

There was a ceremony — a celebration at the end with speeches, congratulations, metals and T-shirts. For me this was a once in a lifetime event. Thank you Sherlene, for introducing me to long distance walking. I never could have done this without you. And thank you, God, for these wonderful friends.

The five, sometimes six of us continued to walk together eventually from 6:30 AM to 8 AM five days a week, three to four miles a day for five years. We had such fun! And we still keep in touch. Friends are such a blessing. I'm going to write mine a note. How about you?

PASTORAL CARE BLESSINGS

As Minister of Pastoral Care, I was the one to receive the requests for emergency calls for a pastor which were received occasionally by our congregation. Several of these were very memorable to me.

One day we had a call from a hospital to see a lady who was on a respirator. I was told she had a debilitating lung condition which impaired her breathing. She had been on a respirator for some time and the decision had been made that the respirator would be removed. When I arrived, I was ushered into the room of a lady on a respirator which meant she couldn't speak. She was pushing a clipboard towards me with funeral written on it. I had the impression something was going to happen momentarily and there was great urgency. She seemed so frantic. I introduced myself. She was writing something about Psalm 121, the Apostles Creed and the Lord's Prayer on the board. When I asked about these, she indicated they were to be in her funeral. Her doctor was coming in and I was asked to stay with her for that meeting. He explained that she could decide when the respirator would be removed. There was no conversation about what would happen at the time it was removed. I was still in shock at this emotional situation and didn't think to ask the Doctor. I surmised that Sharon expected that would end her life. No date was decided at this time.

After the doctor left, I sat down, the tension decreased, and we began to become acquainted with the help of her clipboard. She was relieved that she would have time to get her last wishes in order.

Sharon was a charter member of Lutheran Church of the Incarnation. She was very proud of this. She and her husband had worked very had helping the church in its organizing phase. Following their divorce, her

110

husband continued on at the church, but she never went back. She had been removed from the membership roles because she didn't participate. She worked for a construction company and had to work weekends. Although she hadn't been going to church, her faith was strong. Every morning she read Psalm 121, confessed the Apostles Creed, and prayed the Lord's Prayer, she told me. She missed her church and was so happy to have this connection now. She wanted her funeral to include Psalm 121, the Apostles Creed, and the Lord's Prayer. She would be cremated, and she wanted the service to be by the ocean with her ashes spread in the sea. I assured her that her wishes would be followed.

She and her son would discuss the date for the removal of the respirator and asked if I would come. I said I'd be happy to be there for her.

As I left the hospital that day my mind was whirling. Just think, someone who has been very active in a church where she was happily engaged to be shut off by divorce. That could have happened to me. It was so difficult to go to church after I'd separated from my husband. And she had kept connected to God by reading one Scripture, clinging to the faith expressed in the Apostles Creed and praying the Prayer — The Lord's Prayer she'd been taught. Thank God she had that. And now at this crucial moment in her life — I think she thought the doctor would turn off the respirator right then! She had someone call to a pastor to reconnect her. What a privilege to be there at that moment, that time for her. It was a God Moment for both of us.

The appointed day came. I came. We had devotions and prayer. The respirator was removed. She kept on breathing on her own. She was surprised, yet fearful of what her end would be. The doctor assured her she would be cared for and supported through those days. She was transferred to a care center in the area.

I enjoyed visiting her over the next few months. We had a chance to talk about what Jesus has done for us: how He came as a baby, so defenseless — God coming into the world as one of us. We read about Jesus' acts of love, His healings, His concern for the marginalized. And we read the Gospel account of Jesus' suffering and death in Luke. How horribly He suffered not for His sins but for ours. We noted that the women were at the cross witnessing his death. They were at the tomb when they buried Jesus, and they found the stone rolled away, the tomb empty, and the two men who told them Jesus was risen. The women tried to tell the disciples, and no one would believe them. Sharon was happy to hear the stories again. It had been a long time since she had heard them. She had not been to church for years, but she knew the pastors' names and had kept up with what was being done there. She was happy to be reconnected. The Pastor came by to visit her.

In the end she had a very peaceful death. The anxiety which she feared was eased by medication. We had her funeral service in the park by the beach with her family and friends. The family took care of her ashes. It was a blessing for me to be able to reconnect her with her church and walk with her there final months. It reminds me and all of us to be ready for our final hour.

Another call came from Anna, a ninety-nine-year-old lady. She was a tiny woman lying in her bed in her home which looked like it had been stripped of all her belongings. She told me she had been the wife of a USA ambassador who had served in the European countries. Her husband had died a number of years before. She had become frail and disabled. Without children or family, she had been cared for by caregivers in her home for some time. Some of her best friends were the local policemen who she had turned to when her belongings had gradually disappeared from her home. Now they stopped by frequently to check on her.

She explained to me that she had been confirmed in the Lutheran Church in the German language when she was a teenager. I told her that was true of my mother also. But unlike my mother, she had not participated in church since then. Her concern was for forgiveness. I asked if she had particular situations that were bothering her and she wasn't interested in naming anything. She knew she had hurt people and sinned through her interactions through the years. She needed forgiveness. We talked about Jesus' promise that if we confess our sin, God will forgive them. I read her other passages showing Jesus' power to forgive sin and heal. I explained that we have a service of confession and forgiveness which I would bring in two days when I worked again, if she liked. I prayed with her and returned as agreed with the service and communion.

My contact with her reminded me of the outreaching love which the Holy Spirit displays to God's people. How many times over how many years was she reminded of her need for God in her life? She responded now when she was old and frail. When she was confined primarily to her bed and the distractions were few. Lord, speak boldly to those who have wandered away.

I visited her every few weeks. She seemed at peace. When she died, several months later, I was asked to do her funeral. We had it in the church. The majority of those few attending were local policemen.

Another emergency call to the hospital brought me to witness the tragic death of Sarah, a forty-five-year-old woman. Her sixteen-year-old son, Dan and Mari, her nineteen-year-old daughter and husband Mark were with her. They were all devastated, especially Mark. Sarah had been on a respirator for some time. Her hands and feet had turned very dark. Now the doctors had advised them that hope for her life was gone and advising that the respirator could be removed. I asked if I could pray with them. They weren't sure they wanted prayer. I stood there praying silently, while my tears flowed along with theirs. God was so present in that room. God was all around them — they were surrounded by prayer. Yet the words weren't spoken there.

They asked me to have Sarah's funeral at Incarnation Lutheran Church because Dan had attended pre-school there.

The family came into my office to plan the service. I showed them the funeral service in the service-hymn book. Mari looked at it. She said they would like a warm, personal service and this one seemed formal and cool. Her mother was a medical technologist working in a lab where she caught strep infection from specimens. Strep toxins killed her. I remember studying about streptococci in nursing school. Never in my forty years as a nurse had I seen anyone dying from a streptococci infection. Yet she was the second woman I had buried dying from strep in my short ministry. Sarah had not been feeling well for several days, then she was hospitalized. She had become infected, toxins began to form in her body, causing respiratory distress, demanding a respirator and eventually her demise. Antibiotics, unfortunately, are not effective against toxins.

Sarah was a vivacious woman, full of life and good will. She danced with the cleaning lady when she came to their home. She gave a birthday party for the custodian at work. She gifted people with flowers and love. Her generosity and presence was life giving. I would have liked to meet her!

We found the Scripture in Isaiah 61:1-3 CEV spoke to their grief: "The Lord has chosen and sent me....to heal the broken hearted....The Lord sent me to comfort those who mourn...He sent me to give them flowers in place of their sorrows, olive oil in place of tears, and joyous praise in place of broken hearts. They will be called 'Trees of Justice,' planted by the Lord to honor his name."

I rewrote prayers in simple language. I knew this funeral would be huge, and I was nervous about doing this service by myself. I asked the Pastor to help. He seemed surprised and reluctant, but he was gracious in assisting me. It went well and the family, especially the daughter seemed pleased. I pray the family found healing and solace.

These situations are with strangers and were special to me because I was called and able to bring them comfort. I'm thankful that I was able to be their help in time of need.

We did a lot of pastoral care in our congregation. It was done not only by me but by the other pastors, the deacons, the Incarnation Friends (IF's) and the nurses as well as individual members serving each other. In Luke 22: 42-43 Jesus prayed in his distress, "Father...and the angel from heaven appeared to him and gave him strength." The deacons, pastors, IF's, nurses and all of us who do pastoral care pray that we can be an angel or maybe just the hands and feet of Jesus as we seek to support people on their Christian journey — support them as Jesus has supported me. Thank you, Lord Jesus for your example.

Maybe you've needed and angel ...or maybe you've been one!

MISSION CALLS

Incarnation had one mission project and they did it very well. For two weeks every winter the social hall was converted into sleeping rooms for homeless families. The people who came were screened by the Interfaith organization and were working with counselors to find employment, meet health needs and other personal challenges. Their goal was to find housing and be able to maintain it. It took coordinators and many volunteers to set up, feed them, give childcare, transportation and provide night attendants.

I wondered if there was interest in global mission work at Incarnation. When I left Epiphany, they said they could no longer help Nkuhungu Lutheran Congregation in Tanzania. I discussed this with the Pastor. He knew several people who had expressed interest in global mission the past. In the fall of my first year, we formed a Global Mission Committee and started planning a Global Mission Sunday for early the next year. We set the date for February 4th, 2001.

We were looking for a missionary speaker. No one I contacted in the area was available. Then I heard that Paul Mwanga from Dodoma, Tanzania, my acquaintance, was in Ohio, studying for a M. A. in Theology. He agreed to come for the weekend and preach on Sunday. Members met him at the airport, hosted him in their home, and toured him around San Diego on Saturday afternoon. He preached at both services on Sunday and talked about Nkuhungu Lutheran Church and their challenges with the AID's epidemic at the Adult Forum during the Education hour. An offering was taken for Nkuhungu that morning.

I had been doing prison ministry at La Mesa Prison in Tijuana, Mexico for about nine months as I will tell about later. Paul was interested in prison ministry, so he stayed until Tuesday so he could go with me. On

Monday morning he and two men from the congregation accompanied me to La Mesa Prison in Tijuana, Mexico. It was the first time for the three men. Even with explanation, it was always a shock to go into that prison. They visited with the Americans and assisted as they were able in distributing the food. It was good to have them there.

The highlight of the weekend for me was the visit I had with Paul Mwanga after the prison visit. He came to my condo and told me of his desire to work with prisoners, widows and children. AIDS was becoming a huge problem — a heterosexual problem in Dodoma. The cultural acceptance of men's extramarital affairs meant that men working away from their families would unknowingly become infected, bring it home and infect their wife. There were many occasions that both parents would die, leaving their children orphans. Many times, the grandparents would take care of them. In some cases, older siblings would take the parent role.

Finances were a huge problem. If the wife became widowed, the deceased husband's family had the legal right to take all the property and assets, leaving the widow destitute. She then was left without resources to provide for herself and her children unless there was a written will with other instructions. Wills were not common. The fact was that women often had no education or training. For them to support themselves and their families was a huge challenge.

Paul said that his bishop was encouraging him to become a pastor. However, Paul felt a strong call to establish a Christian non-profit agency to help prisoners, widows and children. He wouldn't have time to do that if he was a pastor. We talked at some length about this and prayed together. I encouraged him to follow his heart and his call. I felt so close to him, I recognized that it was very unusual for a Tanzanian to establish run a non-profit. I was very encouraged by that. Paul and I kept in touch by email.

117

I tried to stir interest at Incarnation Lutheran to help support Nkuhungu Lutheran. One member of the mission committee had previous ties with mission work in Madagascar and thought they should support work there. The chairperson became ill and the committee became less active. The next year the Pastor planned a mission Sunday.

For the first six months at Incarnation I wore a clerical collar to work every day. They hadn't had a woman pastor for a number of years and I wanted to be recognized as a pastor. One day I was wearing a crocheted clerical collar that I had purchased from an Amish lady when I was on internship. Maggi, a member of the congregation saw it and got very excited! She loved to crochet and asked if she could crochet a copy of it. She could crochet it by looking at it, she said. That was exciting for me also. And I was very surprised. I reflected on the two women in Iowa who told me that they had worked all winter on the one-hundred-year-old pattern and only Marie was successful in completing the collar. Marie tried to make another for me and it wasn't as nice, but I gave it to my friend and she enjoyed it.

Now Maggi said she could crochet the collar and she did! She also shaped the shoulders so it fit better, and she improved the band on the neck so it looked more like a clerical collar. It was great, and I enjoyed wearing it. And Maggi said she could make a pattern, so others could crochet it.

I kept reflecting on the women I had talked to in Tanzania who wanted to go to seminary but couldn't afford it. They would apply for scholarship money, but the money was given to the men. The women couldn't afford seminary.

The Tanzanian women liked to crochet. Could they follow a pattern to make the collar, send them back to the US to market them to female pastors? The money could be used to help the seminarians.

The collar pattern looked good. Maggi crocheted two collars. I contacted the crochet guild of San Diego. Several women looked at the pattern. They couldn't follow it. I knew how to crochet a little but had never worked with string. It was too complicated for me. My friend, Linda's sister liked to crochet. She was sent a pattern, but she was unsuccessful. Maggi and I worked on this for about four months. One day Maggi said she had met a man on the internet and she was going to move East and get married. The mission collar project ended but I was thoroughly enjoying my clerical collar. It was an exciting try!

I'll always remember the time when I first looked at the collar with Marie, it's creator. I was thinking out-loud, "Can I use this for a clerical collar?" Marie said, "Those others are made for men! This one looks beautiful on you. You should have a feminine collar!" I loved it and I wanted other women to have the option of having it too.

Maybe more important was the prison ministry with the congregation's involvement. The women making sandwiches, some of the men going with me as I explain elsewhere: this was truly DOING mission work. And it continued after I left as George continued there. Donations from the congregation were $300-$400 per month providing personal care items and food.

THE OPPOSITE OF GRACE

From the beginning, working with my pastor brought challenges. The Sunday I was installed, after the services, I was summoned to his office because one of the deacons told the pastor that he was unhappy with something I had said at our deacon's meeting. This was so important to the pastor that it had to be discussed for thirty minutes after the Sunday services when he knew I had a house full of out of town visitors. It seemed like the pastor was putting me on notice that he was in charge and I was not to make any problems for him. I also got the message that I couldn't depend on him to support me. I had been cautioned by my predecessor that some of the deacons felt very special and this deacon apparently very special.

My internship supervisor and Pastor Washington had both been so gracious, reassuring me that one could make mistakes, be oneself in leading the service and the liturgy. Not so here, anger and scolding met every variation from perfection. I really missed the graceful atmosphere.

The ministry I was doing the first year and a half at Incarnation was very exciting for me. I led the spiritual section of council retreats, got acquainted with my pastoral care volunteers and taught classes on prayer. This led to beginning a Centering Prayer Group. I also started a weekly healing service. On my time off I volunteered with prison ministry, which transitioned into my being in charge of the Monday prison visits and services there when the chaplain began an advanced study program. I brought this ministry into the congregation asking for their sponsorship and participation.

On my first annual review in the fall of my first year, I was told that I was the breath of fresh air that they needed. They were so happy to have me there.

I was certainly aware of pastor's need for recognition and praise. Early on he demonstrated that to me by writing a fake newsletter article as if written by me, praising him. It was presented as a joke. I laughed, wrote a little note praising him. This too was a joke, but he was so happy. He danced around and came into my office, placed a kiss on my cheek, (shock!) saying we would have many years of doing ministry together. Although the Apostle Paul said he could be all things to all people (1 Corinthians 9:22), I failed in that assignment. I tried to be complementary to pastor but giving effluent praise didn't feel right to me. I thought God calls us to be who we are.

I saw so many opportunities to do ministry and I had energy to do them. Each one was done with pastor's permission. The pastor was leading the development of a baptismal font on the patio as a memorial to a member. The assistant was quietly trying to redefine his position from youth minister to focus on education and starting an alternative worship service.

I don't know what prompted it but in June 2001 I wrote a note to pastor about hymns that appealed to the heart versus intellectual "head" hymns. The note wasn't meant to be critical. It might just have been because I was missing the "heart" connection in our formal worship service.

Pastor was so angry! He stormed into my office, his face red, his eyes wide. With the note in his hand he said, "What am I supposed to do with this? Is Margie getting enough attention? Are Margie's needs being met?" He said I was narcissistic, always wanting what I wanted, always knowing what is best for this congregation. "I'm not the only one who thinks this. Members of the congregations do too. I tell them, don't tell me, tell her.

This isn't your kind of congregation. You aren't happy here. What are you doing here anyway? What are you here to learn?" He went on, putting me down, demeaning me. Was he trying to scare me off? Trying to keep me in my place? I had a tear in my eye, not down my face.

I couldn't figure out what he was so angry about. I wondered if he was threatened by me. He certainly thought I was trying to get attention. He didn't like my suggestions/comments about evangelism. Only now do I think I've figured it out. It was his birthday which I wasn't aware of. He opened the note, expecting praise and got a note about evangelism and all of his frustration poured out. What an ugly temper!

Then he sat there and said, "But there are things I really like about you. No one is going to deter you — you're going to stick with your beliefs, be yourself."

He was going on vacation for a month. I asked to revisit this when he returned, and he blew it off. He said he was done with it, putting it behind him and moving on.

The pastor had told me his wife wouldn't listen to him, told him to go and cool off. That's what he was talking about, his temper.

My annual review was the next day. I wondered how much of this I should share with the committee. My daughter advised me to share. I prayed. I shared. No one on the committee had heard anything about me knowing it all or having a superior attitude. One member said that he thought pastor had never had anyone around with challenging ideas, who said what they thought! The pastor had told the committee last month that he wanted a female Ron Horn (the non-clergy that was my predecessor) and that isn't what he got!

The committee encouraged me strongly to be myself. Keep writing notes on evangelism. They were so glad I was here. I have contributions to make — bringing new ideas, sharing what I know. Just being me!

I spent a lot of time praying about this encounter and looking at the process, trying to forgive. I got a cold and my asthma began flaring up.

When he returned, I was very cautious of him and he of me. I attempted to talk to him about it eventually, but he wasn't cooperative. He said that is the way he is. Accept it and move on. He's reacted that way to others and now they are his friends. He sent the associate to tell me I should leave. I thought I had ministry to do here and felt I should stay. That fall I had the worst episode with a cold and asthma that I've ever had. I took several series of antibiotics but the cold just didn't clear for several weeks. Then after a couple of months I had the big baptismal service at the prison, became very sick and a spot on my lung. The test for tuberculosis was falsely reported as positive and the pastor complained about me to the assistant to the bishop. My volunteering at the prison was interfering with my ministry at Incarnation, he said. My lungs cleared but the situation did not. In July, I recognized I needed to leave this parish. I made an appointment with the bishop, explaining our situation. He understood, saying he had been in a similar situation at on time. Put in your resignation, preach your last Sunday and try not to involve the congregation.

At this time, I became aware that the council was discussing the pastoral conflict. The president came to talk with me. I explained that I was planning to leave but since I didn't have retirement strategy would appreciate some help for a few months. They were very gracious, and I resigned four weeks later.

I gave my resignation to the pastor and told him I'd like to preach my last Sunday. Again, he stormed into my office telling me I couldn't preach. He was doing a preaching series and it couldn't be interrupted. "I went to talk to the bishop who told me I should preach my last Sunday." I said.

"You weren't called to preach! I'm the preacher here!" He yelled. His face was so red! His eyes popping.

"I was reading the constitution of this congregation this morning, I wish I had read it earlier." I pulled it out." It says here that all called ordained pastors in this congregation are to teach, preach, and baptize. This would have helped us in our previous discussions about allowing me to preach once a quarter." He stormed out.

Five minutes later he was back with more blasting. Back and forth again finally saying I could preach. Angry, angry, angry. I was calm and said, "Please sit down." And I closed the door. He did. "We need to talk," I said.

And we talked for about thirty minutes. He has been afraid of me and I of him. I don't give in and that was new to him. He said he didn't know why I was here. I said I read a story on internet just a day or so ago about and ant and a contact lens. I had a copy of it and read it to him.

The young woman was rock climbing on a difficult granite cliff. She was taking a breather on a ledge when the rope snapped against her face and her contact lens flew out. She was very dependent on her contacts, she tried to find it there but was unsuccessful. She made it to the top and sat down to wait for the others.

She looked out across the range of mountains, thinking of the Bible verse that says, "The eyes of the Lord run to and fro throughout the whole earth." She thought, "Lord, you know every stone and leaf. You know exactly where my contact is. Please help me."

Finally, they walked down the trail to the bottom. Someone called out, "Did anyone lose a contact lens?" One of their group had seen an ant slowly carrying this load on its back. The girl's father, a cartoonist made a cartoon with the ant lugging that contact lens with the words, "God, I don't know why you want me to carry this thing. I can't eat it and it's awfully heavy. But if this is what you want me do, I'll carry it for you."

"I don't know why God wanted me here, but I felt called. And now I'll be going. I'm sorry if I've caused problems for you," I said. He sort of apologized. And he left my office. I preached my last Sunday and left Lutheran Church of the Incarnation with a smile on my face.

I had a very difficult time releasing the image of that angry face. The thought of moving and starting all over again in a new parish seemed like an overwhelming task, one that I was unable to handle. I was crushed, and I needed time to heal.

Have you ever wondered why you have been put in a certain position?

PRISON MINISTRY
SECTION V

MY GIFT TO YOU

The doors clanged behind us as we moved into a crowd of men in a large cemented yard. Welcoming us to La Mesa Prison was a group of men who warmly greeted the chaplain with half hugs and smiles. I was introduced, and we threaded our way along a very busy path lined with booths like a small market. I was struggling to stay close to the chaplain in this seemingly hostile environment.

As we walked, two women joined us, and we tried to have a conversation in English. Suddenly another door clanged shut, and I was on the outside with my new women companions, Harriet and Agnes. The rest of the group had entered the cell block. We rattled the gate, but the response was not imminent.

Beside me was a man, with syringe and needle in hand. He managed to get the tourniquet on his bare arm. "Stop that!" Harriet shouted. "Have some respect. Can't you see she's a pastor?" The needle entered his vein, and the drug was injected.

I stood there dazed, trying to carry on a conversation with the women.

After a time, which seemed like forever, someone came from inside with a guard, and we were escorted to the cell, already chuck full, but they made room for us.

These were United States citizens in La Mesa Prison in Tijuana, Mexico, accused of a variety of infractions. Each person, after various run-ins with Mexican authorities, were incarcerated here, most awaiting trial. The cell was paid for by the chaplain's ministry. Yes, it had to be paid for. Here eight men lived. Safe behind the cell's door – guilty until proven innocent under Mexican judicial system —no easy task.

They had had check-in, and now the chaplain was having devotional time in the cell. There was discussion of community and personal issues with the Americans. We went out weaving through the crowd again single file to a large room where the chaplain had a worship service. This was open to all prisoners wishing to attend. Chaplain had a sixty-minute preaching-teaching, Bible-thumping sermon. We sang songs. There were about 15 Americans with about 50 Mexicans attending. Following the service, the bread which we had brought was distributed. This was greatly appreciated.

It was an amazing day for me. Riding with the chaplain, we visited a food pantry in south San Diego, where we picked up bread and a few other food items. We stopped for lunch before crossing the border. Experiencing the border crossing, we then proceeded to the prison. There was another lengthy process of getting in. The visit and service were the highlights, followed by waiting with others in a room where the guards would allow people to leave, a long line at the border to work though and fifty miles home.

This was my first visit to La Mesa Prison. The chaplain asked if I'd go with him each week to minister to the women. I delayed a decision.

My prayer was, "God, you don't want me to go there, do you?" I was scared. I had thought of prison ministry in the past. My father was in prison, and I had visited once as a child. It was not like this! As a public health nurse, I went to the county jail several times to do nursing procedures like changing dressings on a prisoner. And as a pastor I had visited a relative of a parishioner at Los Angeles County Jail. I had not seen a prison like this before.

I thought back through this experience and I prayed, "Please, tell me you don't want me to go there." My prayers continued for several weeks.

One day when praying, I saw two hands extended to me holding a lovely wrapped box with a ribbon on it. I heard a voice say, "This is my gift to you! Will you go to the prison for me?"

God was offering me prison ministry as a gift! I would never have thought of this ministry as a gift from God. Go for God? How could I refuse? How would this ministry bring delight and joy as gifts often do? Had my other experiences with prisons not prepared me for this volunteer assignment? My half-time call allowed me adequate time. My parish call was in an affluent community. How would this affect my parish ministry?

Of course, I accepted God's gift to me. I went to La Mesa three times a month for about two years. And these visits opened new experiences, new relationships, new understandings of God, and blessings galore.

ALL KINDS OF PRISONS

"Do you know what I learned at La Mesa today, Chaplain?" I said as we were driving back to San Diego.

"No."

I learned that the guards tell the prisoners to meet them at one place and then go to a different location, so the inmates have to hunt for their guard to check-in."

"I've heard that too."

"And I also heard that if they don't report for check-in, (i.e. they don't find the guard) they're punished by being put in a detention room."

"Unfortunately, that's the system here," he said.

"Is it true that next door to the detention area there is a room with a cot in it where they can sexually assault the men as their punishment?"

"That's what I've been told."

"I find that very shocking. The detainees here don't even have control over their own bodies!"

We were both quiet for a while. I was thinking about Chaplain's sermon today. His theme was "KEEP YOUR BODY PURE AND HOLY," based on Romans 12:1. "Present your bodies as a living sacrifice to God, holy and acceptable to God...what is good and acceptable and perfect," with many other Bible passages.

Knowing he was in charge yet feeling a need to talk about my new information and his approach, I reopened the conversation. "Regarding your sermon today, I know it's important to take care of our bodies because God honors purity and holiness. It's a tremendous challenge for the people here to do that but even more so when they can be abused at the will of the guards. I wonder if there is a way to teach about this while being sensitive to their realities. What do you think?"

"Maybe you would like to preach about that next week," he said.

"Well, yes, I can do that," I said, so surprised!

I had been coming along to the prison several months. Never before had my preaching been mentioned. Ministering to the women was what I had been invited to help with. There were a half dozen or so American women there, and I had made efforts to spend time with them but there was little interest on their part. There was no effort to provide them with a safe place, a cell as the men had, so it seemed that in order for them to exist at La Mesa they had to be linked up with a man for safety.

My time there always included the service conducted by the Chaplain. I had been listening to Chaplain preaching. His sixty-minute sermons in English were based on a topic, usually one key verse with other singular verses to support the theme which were from the New Testament Epistles on Christian living, much more law than gospel. His style was animated, raising his voice, jumping up on the chair sometimes, swinging his arms, moving about. As he called out verses, he was finding them in his Bible to read them. On the other hand, his audience of about fifty mostly men, Americans and Mexicans, sat quietly in their chairs, many nodding off, some staring off with a far-away gaze with little reaction. His was a style of preaching I'd rarely heard—certainly not my tradition.

Chaplain had shared with me that his was a Baptist tradition. He had worked in an Evangelical church where the pastor did not believe in women in ministry. He had been discharged from that church because he had previously had a woman working with him in the prison. His own view was that women could be ministers but only under the direction of a male pastor. He was now employed as a chaplain at the local hospital with prison ministry as his volunteer commitment which he has been doing for six years. His interest stemmed from his own experience in prison where he had experienced conversion.

What was it like to live behind these bare at walls La Mesa Prison? How can these people find the freedom that Jesus promised? Jesus said he was sent to proclaim freedom to all people. Here there was the threat of sexual assault and drugs. Sometimes the guards would throw down individual doses of drugs from a balcony, I was told, encouraging drug dependency.

This seemed like a very boring place to be. The only responsibility the inmates had was to report for check-in to their guard morning and evening. There were very few or no activities, no work, no reading materials. They had to occupy themselves — with what? There was little food and rarely visitors. Ours was a ministry of presence. They were so happy that we cared enough to come. Perhaps Monday visits by the chaplain and whoever he brought along were the highlight of the week.

And now I was planning my first sermon there. I prayerfully reflected on scripture. This was an interesting experience for me because I was accustomed to following a prescribed plan. I chose Isaiah 61:1-4, the text that Jesus read in the temple, saying "Today this Scripture has been fulfilled in your hearing." Romans 8:1-6, when we believe in Jesus, we are free of the law of sin and death. The Gospel Mark1:29-34, Jesus healing. My theme was "Made Free."

I started talking about the many kinds of prisons there are, such as La Mesa, the prison of addiction and the kind that abuse creates. I told them I grew up in a home where I was sexually abused by my father. It was a prison of abuse, a prison of silence. There were threats and power. No one to help. Attempts to make it look normal but so miserable.

I explained that Jesus came to free us from these prisons. Not that the doors of La Mesa would be open for them but by believing in Jesus we can ask for forgiveness from our sins and Jesus would forgive us. It doesn't take away the legal punishment, but the heavy load is gone. We are free of guilt. Our spirits are free. God loves us and sent Jesus as a human like us to teach us how to love—how to live—and to free us from fear and death.

I talked more about the scriptures and God's love for us. I felt every eye on me for that 15- minute sermon. When I finished all fifty of them arose to their feet and clapped! A standing ovation. My first and only one. I was so surprised.

On the ride back to San Diego, the Chaplain said, "I guess you do have something to share with them."

What a blessing for me! I could share my life with them and connect with them which made it very special. After a few months, Chaplain was taking some advanced training and was required to be in class on Mondays. He asked me to take over the Monday visits. He would continue to visit at another time centering on connecting with relatives, handling money issues and other aspects of his ministry there.

HALLE

It was the day after Easter, and we were at the food shelter in downtown San Diego. This is where the chaplain came each week to pick up food to take to the prison. Food was so appreciated. We heard from the inmates that they were served only two meals a day — thin gruel in the morning and a watery broth soup with an occasional piece of potato or vegetable and a tortilla later in the day. Everyone was hungry. This made drug use attractive, to ease the pain of hunger and boredom.

One room at the food shelter was for bakery — bagels and rolls that were highly sought after —and doughnuts and sweet rolls. They would come in boxes or large plastic bags, day old, or more often removed from the shelves in the stores. And then there was fruit in a large outdoor room with apples, oranges, peaches, or whatever was in season.

This day I saw a little kitty, white with orange and black on the head and paws, scampering among the boxes with mommy right behind. So tiny was she, along with several siblings, and so pretty I just couldn't get my eyes off of her. I picked her up and held her in my hands. Suddenly I wanted her to come home with me. Could I manage a kitty? "She's ready to leave," I was told. The kittens were six weeks old, and they were looking for homes for them. A lady who was a volunteer chaplain with us, offered to care for the kitten when I traveled. That helped me decide I could accept this responsibility. She became my Easter Hallelujah, nicknamed, Halle. What a blessing she was! I sang to her, "Halle, Halle, Halle, lu-i-a; Halle Halle Halle-lu-i-a. Halle Halle, Halle, lu-i-a, Hallelujah, halle-lu-ia!"

The first visit was to the vet where she was checked over, passed with flying colors, and given initial shots. Halle was so shy at first. She'd hide under the bed where I had difficulty getting her. But she knew how to drink milk, and thankfully she understood what the litter box was for. From the very beginning, never an accident! We learned how to play together. A string holding a bell from the rocking chair rung with great fun. And we could play ball. There were toy mice, feathers, and other toys.

I read somewhere that some cats liked to go for walks on a leash. We tried that a few times —not fun for her. I thought since she was born and raised outside that I should let her out on the patio. One time she went under the fence to the neighbors, went under her picnic table and frightened her guest who was afraid of cats. That wasn't working very well. So, a leash was necessary sometimes.

Halle was a wonderful companion. She slept on my bed unless I was restless. Often if I had overnight guests, she'd roam during the night to visit them. She followed me to the kitchen and wherever I went in the condo. When I had guests, she would hide but gradually sneak out and make her way to their purses trying to get in them.

Her curiosity was to be admired as she climbed window sills, fireplace mantle, and thoroughly cased the condo. I tried to keep her off the table and kitchen cupboards with sticky tape and a few other tricks. I was quite successful.

She liked to bring me surprises. She brought me a live mouse that had gotten into my piano. Thank you, but no thanks. One day with the patio door open, I came into the living room, hearing an unfamiliar fluttering sound. What was it? Halle was lying on the carpet. I looked around and there in a deep, aqua flower vase on the window sill was a fluttering bird — a humming bird! — struggling to get out. Halle had brought it in for me! I thanked her and helped the beautiful bird escape back to its

135

environment. Isn't it amazing that a cat could catch a hummingbird and bring it in unharmed? The mouse wasn't harmed either.

My friend took care of Halle when I went to visit my exchange daughter in Japan. She wasn't home when I returned, so I couldn't pick her up on my way from the airport. I came home and did my exercises on the carpet that night. At work the next day, I started itching. Lesions developed on my ankles, going up my legs and scattered to my torso. My legs started swelling. Calls to my allergist's office were unsuccessful. I headed to urgent care. Flea bites! The fleas had been multiplying in my carpet during those hot days Halle and I were gone. A cortisone regime helped my bites, but I had to deal with the carpet. I wasn't feeling very well the next day, and Bev, a lady from church, came with chicken soup and Borax. She helped me sprinkle the Borax on the carpet and work it in. I was on the mend and now the fleas were under control. What an angel!

That was my introduction to cat fleas in California. Halle had picked them up in the outside spaces. We had a cat in Minnesota for years but never a flea. No freeze — they multiply! When I picked up Halle from my friend's, she said, "Oh, yes, I noticed she had fleas, so I treated her." Regular treatment routine was followed.

What a beautiful kitty! I thought she was a calico but found a picture in a cat book that called her a Turkish Van—white body, the head and tail with orange and black spots, and up to two colored spots on the body. The book said this breed liked water. Not Halle! She kept herself so clean and bright white but didn't like water.

What a disappointment when after five years, I had to find a new home for her. I wanted to travel and couldn't find proper care for her. A friend in Los Angeles was looking for a companion and happily opened her home to Halle. Sadly, I said goodbye to this blessing from La Mesa.

LA MESA TRANSITIONS

It was a lovely day in September when I drove to La Mesa with volunteer, Alice, to begin my new phase of ministry. This was the first time I was driving to La Mesa. The Monday program would now be mine. I remembered when I first started visiting the prison six months earlier an inmate had said to me, "I suppose you'll be coming by yourself soon?" I must have looked surprised because it was a shocking idea! I had thought to myself, not on your life! But answered, "I don't think so." As the visits and months progressed, I became more comfortable and now I anticipated this change.

And here we were parking the car on the street. Alice, a Native American, met me along the way and was coming to help with a children's program. We stood at the desk, seeking admission. "You're not on the list!" We were told. The chaplain had promised to have my name added to a list of those approved for admission, but it wasn't there. There was no way that the guards would let us in, we were told. There was no higher authority to appeal to. There was no way. We returned to the car, said a prayer and returned home.

The prison definitely felt like a man's world. Our contact with the guards was always so brief. Different guards checked our ID's, searched us, opened the door to let us into the prison, another the door to the cell block and the cell itself and a different one let us out. When we were ready to leave, we entered a waiting area and it seemed like it took a bribe (which I never gave) to get out as we would wait there for 15 minutes to a half hour before they would allow us out the door. There was little opportunity to establish a relationship with them or get to know them personally. While in the prison, it was the Americans who were our protectors and ushered us around. Maybe the struggle of getting in and waiting for them to let us out left no energy to work on relationships with the guards.

The chaplain gave a sincere apology, assuring me he would take care of getting my name on the list and he did.

I had another week to work on the transition. I searched the Internet and church websites looking for material on prison ministry—Bible study guides, sermon suggestions and information on doing prison ministry. Not too successful. I was also concerned that my audience for the service was eighty percent Mexican and many could not understand English. Spanish wasn't in my vocabulary, but prayer was.

I returned the next Monday alone. Alice's car wouldn't start. My name was on the list. I was greeted by John who informed me the electricity was off, so he escorted me to a gathering spot outside where I met the Americans. The visit and service went smoothly.

For about a month I used the Gospel reading for the week as my service topic, then decided to center a series on Baptism. The Chaplain came several weeks later and took over with no hesitation. He came again after a couple of weeks. I said, "I didn't know you were coming." He said, "I suppose you have something prepared." I said, "Yes I do and I don't preach as long as you so I'll be first." And I did. He preached second and never came again on Monday.

By then I had started the series on Baptism. Chaplain wrote me a letter saying I could no longer be under his ministry because I was teaching Lutheran theology of baptism. That shook me up for a short time until I could see what a blessing it was. He would no longer feel he had to supervise me, and I was free to manage this ministry. I could ask my congregation to be my sponsor. I approached my senior pastor, brought it to the council who voted to support La Mesa Prison Ministry.

It was then that I could ask for volunteers, men, to accompany me to the prison. The women were asked to make sandwiches and happily agreed. We set up a fund for prison ministry, asking for donations. The money would be used for transportation expenses, car insurance in Mexico which I purchased weekly until I finally checked to find it unnecessary. I contacted a doughnut shop where they were happy to give us their day-old bakery. And I purchased fruit. Eventually we set up a fund to help pay for showers. On occasion donations of shoes and clothing were delivered.

I decided that my worship services would include the sacrament of the Altar—the Lord's Supper. I remember going to the thrift store to find a plate and chalice. It looked like it might even be silver. It didn't last long—I got distracted at the end of the service talking with someone and the communion set disappeared. I also lost my Bible, the one I had used through seminary with all my notes. How careful you had to be—hanging on to your things. It was a transition, adjusting to prison ministry.

Seventeen men requested baptism when we finished that five-week series. We celebrated with them. Volunteers were coming each week, first the volunteer chaplain then men of the church. One volunteer was a former prisoner in a US prison. I had heard about him. Before I arrived, he had responded one Sunday when the associate pastor had asked if anyone had something they were thankful for. He stood up and said, "I'm so thankful to be out of prison!" This upscale congregation were quite amazed! And in time, he became a leader in the congregation. The ride down and back, and our time with the prisoners made a wonderful day as I heard of his experiences in an American prison and his developing faith.

139

One of our deacons, George, became very interested in this ministry. He began coming every week, so friendly and caring for the inmates, helping with collecting supplies, and sharing ideas of how to make the ministry more effective. He was a realtor—in fact mine, he helped me purchase my condo. He was well organized, and greatly focused on attaining his goals. And one of his goals was to witness to his faith. He shared in the ups and downs of witnessing in this challenging place. On a number of occasions, we would both be quite discouraged as we rode back to San Diego, wondering if our efforts were of any significance, why we were doing this. And by Monday morning we were ready to go—up for another visit to La Mesa. What a blessing and great partner in ministry he was!

At the same time, I was working on a crocheted women's clerical collar project. My senior pastor shook his head. Who is this woman pastor? Working on a lace clerical collar and doing prison ministry at La Mesa Prison, Mexico, known as the second worst prison in the world?

AWESOME GOD

La Mesa covered two square blocks and was built to house 3000 inmates, however 7000 packed the interior. It was a "city within a city" with small shops and eating places. It operated under corrupt supervision where graft and drug-trafficking was a way of life. If you had money you could rent a cell, buy food, pay for a shower. If not, and most of them didn't have money, you slept on the cement slab, outside with no protection, no place to be but in the crowd. This is the prison where Americans were sent when arrested in Tijuana, some falsely accused or set-up, waiting during the long, drawn-out process of proving themselves innocent. Our ministry was primarily to those Americans, but the worship service was open to anyone wishing to attend with fifty to sixty participating. I had preached one time and received a standing ovation. The chaplain thought I had something to offer. I accompanied the chaplain for about six months when he asked if I'd take over the Monday program as he was beginning advanced study that made him unavailable. More comfortable now, I began a new phase of ministry, sponsored by my congregation.

Several months later George, a faithful volunteer from my congregation and I were in the prison reception room. I couldn't find my car keys and I didn't have my I.D. card.

It was the usual Monday morning—getting up early to write the Bible Study for this week for the prisoners and to complete the sermon. There was a short time in the church office where I made copies of the Bible study. And how wonderful again to pick up the 80 sandwiches from the refrigerator that the church women had prepared for us.

George met me at the church, and we then proceeded to the shop to pick up the day-old doughnuts. How the inmates loved them! And off to La Mesa! We stopped for a cheeseburger at Burger King and on to the border crossing. Today the lines were long but inched along and finally were checked through without concern.

As usual, I was fortunate to find a parking spot on the street not too far from the Visitor's entrance. George was out. I popped the trunk and he began taking out the sandwiches, doughnuts, as well as oranges I had purchased. I was busy collecting the ministry supplies for communion, song sheets, Bibles, and Bible Studies. And there I was inside the prison's visitors' reception room with no I.D. — no keys. I thought of going back to the car, but it was always an ordeal to get in and as I thought about it, I was a little afraid of what might be involved to straighten out that situation. So, when the attendant, recognizing us, offered to allow me in on George's identification, (I couldn't believe he offered that!) I decided to resolve it later. We were searched and in time, allowed to go into the prison.

In the cell, the guys were telling us that they were helping with electrical wiring for the prison. "We're going to be able to get up on the roof later today. Actually, up there without fetters! Bring a car around" they joked, "Leave it running and we'll just get off the roof, hop in and get out of this place!" We all had a good laugh.

I told them that I was missing my keys and hadn't been able to figure out where they were. As we had devotions and prayer in the cell, I prayed that God would help resolve that situation.

Three hours later, we arrived at the car. Surprise! The car was running with the keys in the ignition! Untouched on the streets of Tijuana—gas gauge on empty. Awesome God! Was I stupid? Yes! In my concentration on getting the supplies and materials organized, I had left the keys in the ignition and the car running! And God protected it! When we are weak, God is strong. Who would believe that a car, unlocked, with its motor running on the streets of Tijuana would be safe for three hours?

I reflected on this experience many times as I thought about my ministry at La Mesa. Previous to this I had prayed for Jesus to go with me, for protection in the prison. Family, friends and congregation were also giving prayer support. I guess I never really considered how deeply God was involved in this ministry. Of course, I needed God for this whole operation: direction for planning, for preaching, writing sermons, working with volunteers, transportation, and as well as my Senior Pastor who was very nervous about me going to Mexico and the prison. This display of protection was so affirming to me, knowing Jesus was with me and protecting even my car. Awesome God!

I told my Senior Pastor about this experience the next day. Pointing his finger in my face, he said, "Don't you ever do that again!" He said he was going to get after George for not taking care of me. I said "Don't you dare go after George. He's a great helper and not responsible for my errors. Besides, God is taking care of me!" He was concerned about my getting in trouble in Tijuana and he'd have to come and rescue me! By God's grace that never happened.

I gave devotions at our regional pastor's meeting a couple of weeks later. After playing the hymn "My God Is an Awesome God," sang by a friend of mine from seminary, I centered on this experience. One pastor afterwards said he left his car running in a parking lot in San Diego. When he came out it was gone. It was found 20 miles away stripped of many parts.

Thank you, awesome God! When I accepted the gift, I wondered if your gift would bless me as gifts often do. You indeed blessed me, not only with your protection but with seeing lives change. One young man whose name was Trigger, told me he didn't need God in his life. I talked to him, suggested he have a different name. He was studying the Bible with his cell-mates. Several weeks later he waved at me saying, "Remember me? I'm a Christian now, my name is Louis." An avowed atheist came to services and was reading the Bible. Another young man became repentant and vowed off drugs when he heard the words of John the Baptist, "Even now the ax is lying at root of the trees; every tree, therefore, that does not bear good fruit will be chopped down and thrown in the fire." (Luke3:9). God's Word is alive and powerful!

You blessed me and my congregation with a glimpse of a different side of the world. You blessed me with a mentor, the chaplain, who introduced me to a difficult site, a faithful coworker, George, and many others who came along for a short time. You blessed me as I wrote Bible studies appropriate for the prisoners. I was blessed in so many ways and I passed those blessings on. Thank you, Awesome God!

Jeff told me when I came that day, "We're having a meeting tonight. Randy is using drugs. We've tried to talk to him. Our rule is no drugs in this cell, but he won't listen. We talked to Chaplain about it, and he said we should take action."

Bill added, "We really feel bad about doing this to Randy. It's a terrible life out there for a young guy like him — well for anyone. But we've tried our darnedest to convince him, and he's just so stubborn! We just have to kick him out."

All the Americans were in a solemn mood as we went to the service.

In my search for material that had been used in prison ministry, I was happy to find "The Uncommon Lectionary for the Un-Churched, Institutionally Unhappy, Spiritually Seeking Public Churches." It has been an effective tool to promote ecumenical conversation. It presumes no basic knowledge of the Bible and covers the Christian story according to church seasons over a one-year period." It was so appropriate for La Mesa.

Today Enrico was translating for me. My message was on John the Baptist, whose ministry was to prepare the way for Jesus. I read from Luke, Chapter 3 about what a tough guy John was, eating grasshoppers and honey, and dressing in animal skins. His preaching didn't mince words either. "You brood of vipers, who warned you from the wrath that is to come. Bear fruit worthy of repentance. Even now, the ax is lying at the root of the trees; every tree that does not bear good fruit is cut down and thrown in the fire." John preached repentance, and the people thronged to him, repented, and were baptized. That call still comes to us today.

The next week I came, and there was Randy, still in the cell. I was surprised. "What happened?" I asked.

Randy said, "I kept hearing that line you read, 'The ax is at the root. Any tree that does not bear good fruit will be chopped down and thrown in the fire.'" His whole attitude changed. When they came to the meeting that night, Randy was repentant and willing to quit drugs. "He's trying," they told me. And equally amazing, the guys heard it. Praise God! Randy heard the Word, and the Spirit moved his heart that day. Rarely do we hear such dramatic results. I was excited, and this experience emblazoned on my heart in a different way that the Word is powerful. It's alive!

There was other evidence of God's actions in the prison population that I became aware of. Jeff shared with me once that he's a much better Christian in prison than when he's out. He was so supportive to our ministry. A new young man who called himself Trigger, told me, "I don't need God in my life!" I spent some time talking with him that day, hearing about his background, telling him about God's love for him, suggesting that he might want a different name. Five weeks later he came to me saying, "I'm a Christian now. Remember when you talked to me? Now my name is Louis." He had been studying the Bible with Jeff, Bill, and the other guys in the cell. He too found that the Word was powerful. That's why it's called "The Living Word."

The Spanish translation was working well. I asked those in the audience who knew English to alert me if they found the translation to be inaccurate.

One day a Mexican, Jose — one of the fellows who had been on drugs and was baptized — came to tell me his story. He said he was having a Bible study group that met every evening. They met in one of the hallways of the cellblock, but the guards were not happy they were meeting. He had about thirty or so men who came. He was asking for prayer and help with material, and I agreed to assist him. How encouraging to see him with the initiative to teach others. Yes, certainly I would help. Using the Uncommon Lectionary Bible readings, I would introduce the topic for the week, then divide the reading between the six days of the week with two introspective study questions for every day. I would print them out each week, a copy for each participant. We found the translation in Spanish from the Internet helped his participants. This was a flourishing study pattern of various sub-groups with leaders for about eight months.

There was much pressure on the people to take drugs, some of it reportedly initiated by the guards. Unfortunately, Jose fell back into drug addiction and his leadership ended. The power of Satan is alive, too.

I continued providing Bible studies in English for the Americans and in Spanish for the Mexicans.

WOMEN VISITORS

When I first began going to La Mesa without the chaplain, I was accompanied by a woman who was a volunteer chaplain at a hospital in the area. She was with me the day I took Halle, my kitten, home and offered to take care of her when I wanted to travel.

She continued to come when the chaplain was taking his classes. Following the service one day, she said, "So many of the Hispanics can't understand English. Maybe you could have someone translate for you as you preach." As we talked about it, we realized that there were those inmates who spoke English very well who could help by translating. As we prayed about it, I decided to try it. Knowing very little Spanish I couldn't evaluate how accurate the translations were, but the Spanish speakers appreciated it and I felt it was an asset to the ministry. Without her encouragement and support, this would possibly not have happened because my model, the chaplain didn't have his sermons translated.

The women of my congregation were very generous and supportive by making sandwiches — eighty of them every week and praying for my ministry. But one brave woman, bucking her husband's disapproval, accompanied me to La Mesa. What a sensitive, caring, adventurous, supportive woman! When she returned, she wrote this poem:

La Mesa

Hundreds crammed like roaches in a trap
Living in the stink of Hell
Forage a life of the "day to day"-
The "pay to stay" - the "compromise your life away".....

148

Women and children and men and their guards,
Humanity from origins unknown,
Sins of their fathers? Or, sins of their selves?
No matter — they suffer alone.

A flicker of light breaks through with a smile,
A shake of the hand brings surprise,
Not all, but many respond to the touch —
Is hope hiding behind a disguise?

Do they think that their God does not enter these walls?
That their lives are not worthy of love?
Special "few" bring the message of hope to the lost,
"All you seek come from Heaven above".

(God Bless Pastor Margie and this ministry and the many searching souls
it touches.)
*"Demons fly amidst the silent drone of agony. This deafening silence is
manifested by the hollow, empty masks of suffering."*

-Mary

Another beautiful woman asked to come with us to our Christmas visit.
She was an intern pastor at the Lutheran Hispanic Mission in Riverside.
"My aunt and uncle invited me for Christmas, but I can go there when we
return," she said. She wanted to celebrate Christmas with us. What a
delight it was to have her join us. She, like all of us was appalled by the
living conditions at La Mesa but experienced the joy of sharing the

149

message of Jesus birth and celebrating with food, laughter and music. She was fluent in Spanish so could converse with the Mexicans and bring a message from her mission which was primarily Hispanic. Her reflection is included in the next chapter "Christmas at La Mesa" which she wrote for the Synod newsletter.

There was a woman, a Catholic nun who lived at La Mesa. She cared for the sick as best she could with limited resources. I met her briefly on several occasions but mostly heard about her and how much she was admired. She and other volunteers, like Alice were striving to aid the children, brought there by the incarceration of the fathers. The whole family would come — the mother would often get a job in the city, leaving the children with the drug addicted father to care for them during the day. Their home in prison was a make-shift room formed by hanging blankets on wires. Volunteers attempted to run school schedules, part time. They established volunteer sponsored feeding programs with very basic meals. All seemed very inadequate.

CHRISTMAS AT LA MESA

Christmas Day was on Monday, our visiting day and that was one day of the year I was assigned to preach at my congregation. What fun it was to tell our people about our ministry at La Mesa. We were serving an affluent community and they were surprised I would choose to volunteer there.

I had opened the ministry to the congregation with an invitation to the men to accompany me and about six of them did. One of the deacons, George came and felt called to come and continued coming—so faithful, so helpful, so supportive. In fact, he continued after I left!

The women were invited to participate by making sandwiches. Every time we went, we found eighty sandwiches in the refrigerator. What a blessing for the hungry people in the prison. All were invited to pray for us and the ministry and/or contribute to a fund which was used to pay for our expenses, purchases of food, supplies and a shower fund (yes, the inmates had to pay to take a shower.)

But Christmas was special. I planned a service including Christmas carols, reading the Christmas story with a homily, and Holy Communion, which of course was translated into Spanish by one of the inmates. A guest today was a student intern pastor for the Lutheran Mission (CCLM) in Riverside. She brought greetings from her people in Spanish. This is what she wrote about her visit:

"On Christmas Day, I went to La Mesa Federal Prison in Tijuana, Mexico with Pastor Margie Olson and two other members of her congregation. I went not that I had so much to offer. My presence was not essential. Except to me. I went to the prison because I was curious. I wanted to see what this place was like; what did it look like from the

inside, what did it sound and smell like. I enter to be able to VISIT the prison.

As a visitor to La Mesa prison in Tijuana, you have the distinct privilege and power to leave the prison and it stayed there in Tijuana. It could remain an experience (a huge experience at that) that I could revisit in my mind, or anytime I chose to visit the prison. The prison could remain 'another world' to me. Another world, that was not mine and that I had located only in Tijuana, Mexico and not in CA, where I live. Or so I had expected.

But times and places get unexpectedly and divinely woven together so that La Mesa Prison could not stay there in Tijuana but ushered up through the threads of community. A brother of one of the women in our CCLM community died last week at La Mesa Prison in Tijuana, He died on the overcrowded vile concrete ground where hundreds sleep huddled together for space and heat. He died in a cold chill, wearing nothing but his slacks; his shoes, socks and sweater all stolen by other prisoners, trying to survive the cold winter night. He did searching for air, as his asthmatic lungs served to drown him.

My visit to La Mesa prison with Pastor Margie Olson was an experience that opened my eyes, expanded my horizons. Yet my visit brought me back, deeper into the reality of the community, here in this place. It is easier to visit and leave behind than to recognize the ways that we are divinely wound together."

At the time I wrote this reflection:

"I went to La Mesa Prison on Christmas Day, because it was Monday. That's what I do on Mondays. I went to be with the people there—The Americans who are imprisoned there, the Mexican prisoners who join us for worship services, maybe because they get some food or maybe because

as they told one of my parishioners, because they like the singing or they love the Lord and like the atmosphere there even though they can't understand all of it. They like to see smiling faces. I went to be with them because in their faces, I see the face of Jesus.

I went that special day, Christmas, to share the 'Good News' of Jesus birth. As about seventy men and a few women gathered in a cafeteria room, we had a service of carols and the Christmas Story and we prayed. We talked about God's love—love so great that would cause God to send God's Only Son as a helpless baby into our sinful world to live with people like us — love that would enfold us if we allowed it. We shared Eucharist. Afterwards we move to another room to a hot meal of ham, mashed potatoes, raw carrots, apples and oranges and a whole trunkful of bread that a thrift store operator gave me on Christmas Eve. We had bags filled with a comb, toothbrush, soap, shampoo, toilet paper, candy, nuts and a razor. Their dessert was chocolate brownies which Daniel, one of the prisoners had baked. Two cartons of Spanish Bibles were distributed. At the door each was given two quarters, that's what it cost to take a shower — yes, it costs for everything including a bed!

It was wonderful having Rachel, George and Judy along that day. What a wonderful Christmas Day!

We left there but there were over seven thousand people—women, men and children behind the walls of that fortress, La Mesa Prison. So many there were cold, hungry, without security of safety, even necessary medications, like the man Rachel spoke of. So many of them are without God. Socially and economically they are so far away from where I live in California. Yet they tie me to life. Theirs is a real world."

A resource for our team at La Mesa was a United States prisoner, Daniel, who lived with his USA prisoner girlfriend in what they called a condo — kitchen, living area, bedroom, bath. It was hard to believe that some could live in relative luxury in a place they had built and furnished within the prison walls. Their condo had a flat roof so when USA prisoners were admitted, they sometimes housed them there on the roof where they'd be safe. Willie had connections with the administration, so he arranged to help us get supplies into the prison. He also got brownie mix and potatoes and have them baked in the kitchen there. We always suspected that Daniel's connection was with the operative drug lords which was substantiated later.

Unique to this situation was the need to not only bring hams for the prisoners but also for the guards who made it possible to bring the food in. Five hams for the guards, six for the prisoners. It was a party — the prisoners wore their same old smelly clothes, but their faces lit up with smiles. Everyone was hungry and anxious for food, yet they gave place to one another with unusual politeness. To them a simple meal was a feast. And small personal care gifts such as soap or shampoo, a candy bar and a shower ticket were received with sincere gratitude.

THE LAST HURRAH

About eighteen months after the first baptismal service, I was seeing a need for a second one. The Americans in the cell were having Bible studies two times a week. I continued to write Bible studies each week and brought eighty copies. The guys took them. I heard that some met together using them in small groups. Others used them individually.

I started a five-week series again, yes, teaching the Lutheran interpretation of Baptism. I was concerned that people here should know that God loved them and wanted a relationship with them, that they could have a Christian community here in the prison, and that when they got out, they could bring that experience to a church on the outside. Being in a community, they could support one another. For me, baptism was the first step. I led a five-week session again, inviting those who wished to be baptized to sign up. We had fifty guys on the list.

I had become acquainted with a Lutheran Hispanic pastor in Escondido, and I asked, and he agreed to help with the service. We purchased Bibles with our prison fund and gave each person a new Bible. It was a celebration day. As part of the service, I baptized each person and gave them a hug. Pastor Luis laid hands on them, prayed for them individually, and gave them a hug, George handed each a Bible, congratulated them, and blessed them. There was a special air of excitement and joy among the participants. We continued the service with the Lord's Supper. After the service, they shared in sandwiches, fruit, and doughnuts.

Fifty people baptized in one service! Oh, yes, I knew that probably many had been baptized before and this was a blessing (we don't believe in rebaptism), but who can withhold from them when they come forward

155

to ask for it, especially in this place? And since I believe that baptism is a work of God, a calling of people into relationship with God, how can I judge? As I left the prison that day, I felt awed by the experience. I felt joyful, excited, full, silently praising God, yet so tired. And my co-workers expressed similar feelings.

Three days later I was sick! Terrible upper respiratory symptoms, heavy breathing as I felt my asthma symptoms returning. It's a blur what really happened — there were doctor appointments, respiratory tests, x-rays showing a spot on my lung, and TB tests which came back positive. By then I was feeling better but was unable to go to work. Positive for TB! No contact with people! The test was repeated and came back a false positive — it was a mistake by the lab. Praise God, I didn't have tuberculosis! I was feeling well, so was back on the job after two weeks.

It was Lenten season going into Holy Week, and I was to preach on Thursday evening which I did. Unfortunately, my senior pastor became very nervous with the diagnosis of TB and the possibility of a prolonged illness. He went complaining to the Synod office because I was doing prison ministry which was interfering with my work at the church. He found a sympathetic ear from the Assistant to the Bishop. She did not contact me, I only heard of this later.

With the TB diagnosis gone, I still had a growth on my lung. With that diagnosis, I called the chaplain saying I was unable to go back to the prison, and he took over the Monday visits. Six weeks later, I had a bronchoscopy, and no growth was found. A follow up x-ray showed that my lungs were clear.

That was the end of my ministry at La Mesa. I hadn't planned it that way, it just happened. It was so abrupt, but it felt right. Like God's timing. I think the chaplain was ready to get back into that ministry. God had indeed gifted me in many ways, and I had tried to be faithful to God's leading. It was also a blessing to my congregation. Those who visited La Mesa with me saw a new reality in the prison. It gave a different opportunity to reach out to the unfortunate. The women seemed so happy to participate by making sandwiches. I came to know that we all are just a mistake away from being in a similar situation. I learned how much we have to be thankful for the training we've had, the homes we've come from, and all the people who have guided us. George not only was a blessing to me, he continued working with the chaplain after I finished.

I failed to contact Pastor Luis after we returned from the service but heard later that he had been quite sick also. It must have been the hugs because George remained healthy.

At the Synod Assembly in May, a pastor spoke who was doing border ministry in Mexico. He was a pastor from Texas who felt called to establish a position with our church to work with the small Lutheran churches along the Mexican border. He and his wife had been traveling in Mexico for several years doing this ministry and was looking for synod support. At break time, I talked to him about the prison ministry I had been doing. He was very interested. I offered to take him to Tijuana to show him the prison, and he asked to go. So, on a beautiful day, we rode to Tijuana. Pastor Bill, his wife, Ann, and I. We were admitted without problem. Several guys came and ushered us in, greeting me warmly. The Americans were playing baseball with a Mexican team and having a great time. We sat in the bleachers watching with the others. Guys would come by to greet me. That was my final farewell. Pastor Bill and Ann couldn't believe I'd come there to do ministry. I am thankful to you God for gifting me with this prison ministry.

PostScript: On August 20, 2002, at 2:30 in the morning, 1,500 heavily armed police stormed Tijuana's La Mesa State Penitentiary and removed the 2,200 prisoners to a new facility in El Hogo where they would receive education and rehabilitation. Forty-five inmates, considered highly dangerous who allegedly ran the prison's flourishing drug trade (Daniel included), were flown to various maximum-security prisons in other parts of Mexico. Bulldozers removed the booths and shops inside the facility and leveled the condos and private living quarters behind the building.

Approximately 3,000 family members were moved out of the building. Children with only an inmate parent were cared for by their social service agency. Only inmates who were awaiting sentencing remained.

The old La Mesa was no more. It had been cited as one of the worst prisons in the world. The Mexican government planned for months for this tremendous take-over. And it was successful. George continued to work with the Americans there. He said it was a different place, more like a prison should be. He called out his group and met with them. George said the most fulfilling time of his life was when he was working in the prison.

GOD MOMENTS ARE STILL HAPPENING
SECTION VI

REVISITING TANZANIA

I was retired and enjoying the sunshine in California. I had found my place in a small congregation, Gethsemane, with Pastor Gloria, who was wonderfully accepting. I was tending flowers in the garden of Gethsemane and was volunteering at downtown First Lutheran where they had a very active program feeding and supporting the homeless people. Twice a week they fed them, 200 or more. And eventually they developed a medical, dental and hospice program as well.

I was in communication with Paul Mwanga, who with his wife and committee had organized a non-profit organization called Amazing Grace. They invited me to help with a weeklong conference for widows of AIDS in Dodoma, Tanzania in July 2004. Paul said women would be coming to Dodoma from throughout Tanzania. He was raising money to provide for their transportation, room and board. That sounded like a very ambitious plan. The meeting would be centered on God's word, calling them to repentance and new life. I was asked to lead three Bible studies and plan, as well as preach at the worship service on Sunday.

I felt so honored to be asked. Surely, I could do this, a new experience — but maybe not so different from what I'd done at council retreats but in a different language and culture! As usual I started with a blank slate. What did they need? They were widows. They had lost their husbands, maybe even their homes. Had they lost their hope? Most probably they had families, little resources, few skills to provide for themselves and their families. And where was God in this if God was a part of their life? How could God help all of them now?

I found the story of Mary and Martha losing their brother, Lazarus, in John, Chapter 11 to be my Gospel lesson. The women had called Jesus to come. Jesus delayed. He waited two days before setting out to Bethany. Both sisters said, "Jesus, if you had been here, my brother wouldn't have died." Jesus talked theology to Martha and cried with Mary. He treated the sisters differently because their needs were different. He heard their confession of faith and raised Lazarus from the dead. HE RAISED LAZARUS FROM THE DEAD! Jesus did miracles. Jesus can do miracles for you. Jesus will give you strength. Jesus will give you courage.

As companion Scripture I used Isaiah 43:1-4 assuring them that God created us, God loves us, redeemed us and calls us by name. Verse four even says God honors us! How we all need to be loved and honored when our loved one had died of this shameful disease, or whenever we're down and out. I could share how God has lifted me up by guiding me, talking to me, answering my prayers, leading me so closely.

The third Scripture I used was in Jeremiah 29:11-14. "Surely I know the plans I have for you, says the Lord, plans for your welfare and not for harm, to give you a future of hope. Then when you call upon me and come and pray to me, I will hear you. When you search for me, you will find me; if you seek with all your heart." This is the help we all need, wherever we are on our path. God had a plan for each of these women and it was for good!

I didn't need to pick a Scripture reading for the Sunday service because Stella, Paul's wife said, "Can we use the story of the widow who was helped by Elisha in 2 Kings: 4? It's a lesson to use what you have that I think would be helpful for them." It sounded good to me.

The participants had a full week of Bible studies from various viewpoints. For example, I pictured Martha as a woman of faith who was an outgoing community leader because she came out to meet Jesus and the Holy Spirit gave her the voice to call Jesus the Messiah, the Son of God,

161

the only one to do so, in the book of John. The Tanzanian male pastor who followed me said Martha was just a complaining, weak woman and discounted her statement about Jesus being the Messiah as anything significant. He went on laughingly talking about the I Timothy text that described young widows as idle, gadding about, gossiping and being busybodies. It seemed he was making fun of them. I, as well as the several other women presenters were trying to lift them up, build hope.

They had heard information about AIDS, about caring for themselves (Many were tested for AIDS). At this time there were various organizations that could help them with small loans, with learning a skill like sewing, making crafts, start a small market, etc. that would provide income for them and their family.

Basing their life on faith in Jesus Christ was the central theme. Saturday morning was devoted to a healing service which included casting out demons. This was a new experience for me other than watching it on TV earlier. But there were those who were writhing on the floor, (people caring for them), others weeping, many voices praying, some on their knees, some quietly whispering. Pastors were laying on hands, praying individually for those who desired. One of the women pastors told me later that demons are readily acknowledged in their culture. Americans have come to her asking for deliverance from demons. They have been relieved of their symptoms by God and her assistance. I'm certainly aware that we in America make strong efforts to explain all our problems with health as illnesses. When you look at alcohol addiction, for example, the urge to drink is so strong and persistent, I've been told. They call it a demon, we call it an illness. Who is right? Maybe it's both.

We designed the Sunday service to strengthen their faith in God's ability to help them in this time of need. They could begin with what they

162

had and trust God to help them. The friends and neighbors were involved. They provided the vessels. The women were encouraged to form a group where they would help one another, offering support and guidance.

Paul told me I was the rich American which helped attract some of the 200 women who came. But I told him I wasn't rich. I wouldn't be handing out money. I felt I had to bring something! I knew the African women liked scarves mostly to tie around their heads. I had a scarf drawer that was bulging. What if I brought scarfs enough for each of them? And Bibles! I knew that many of them didn't have their own Bible. Could they even read? I set out to ask for donations of scarves — used ones were fine if they were in good condition. And if they could, I'd appreciate a money donation of $5 (for one Bible) or more to help me purchase Swahili language Bibles in Tanzania from the Bible Society. At first, I thought I'd buy Bibles only for those who didn't have one but realized they all would want a new Bible. My friend, Gerri, gave me $100 so with other donations, I had money enough and a 40-inch suitcase filled with over two hundred silk, rayon, cotton scarves of all colors. One donated scarf came in a sealed plastic bag with the note that said, "This was my mother's scarf. I sealed it because it still smells like her." The women loved them.

It was a wonderful women's retreat. And Paul raised the money, several thousand dollars to pay for their food and lodging. I think many struggled to get their transportation paid. I stayed on to visit AIDS patients, AIDS widows and families in distress. I also met people from many agencies that were there to help.

Nkuhungu Lutheran Church invited me to preach and be their guest on the first Sunday I was in Tanzania. I was thrilled to be able to return there. I asked to visit the church on Saturday. When I arrived there were children playing outside. Another group were in the classroom. The organization,

Compassion, International was there supporting one child of each family with school tuition, school uniforms, daily lunches and Saturday Christian program. The church was alive with activity. In the sanctuary the choir was practicing for the service on Sunday. This beautiful brick building stood there where the outline had been seven years earlier. Besides the sanctuary was an education unit. It was quite amazing.

I went back to my room to work on a sermon. The appointed texts for the day included Psalm 66:1-9 which tells us to praise God for being awesome, for doing awesome deeds! That's exactly how I felt after witnessing the activities at Nkuhungu that morning. What an awesome God who had helped these people build this beautiful church and respond to the health crisis. I felt like this Scripture was written especially for our situation today.

A second text was Isaiah 66:10-14, quite a different scene. Here Jerusalem is described as a healing, nurturing, playful mother and then switches in verse 13 to God being that comforting mother image. The sermon used both images of God and I could commend them for how they were stepping up to nurture the children in their community who were in such dire need.

The pastor was new to me. They had changed pastors three times since I first visited. No one on the council remembered me. They gave me a letter of appreciation addressed to Margie Olson in Ohio. Without a map of the United States, it was difficult to help them understand, but we worked on trying to establish my identity as being from California. They gave me a cross for my congregation which was too large for me to carry back and some smaller items which I appreciated greatly. I was delighted to be asked to help them plant an evergreen tree in the church yard. I wonder if it's still there.

The God Moments for me were seeing their church and experiencing the Scripture which was so appropriate for that day. The pastor said he had never heard that Scripture about God as a mother and asked for a copy of my sermon. God as Mother is a favorite for me. Of course, we know that God isn't Father or Mother, God doesn't have gender but is a Spirit. So, I think if we have to assign gender it should be both Father and Mother.

HEALING IN THE PARISH

I moved back to Minnesota in August 2006, locating in Hopkins, just a few blocks from my youngest daughter, Jane and family. It was coming home! I bought a small home with a large lot where I planted fruit trees, flowers and vegetables. I found various community and church opportunities to volunteer. The housing market had fallen drastically at the time I was attempting to sell my condo and it seemed like the best plan was to rent it for a time. This left me short of cash, so I officiated at weddings at the wedding chapel at the Mall of America, put a bathroom in my basement and rented out a room there.

In 2008 All Saints Lutheran had an associate pastor who was on leave of absence for an indefinite period of time. That is my daughter's church and I worshipped there with them when visiting here from California. Christmas was coming with its heavy ministry load. I told Jane to tell Pastor Tim I was available if he needed help. A week before Christmas he called asking if I'd come by to talk about helping out there.

I would assist with the Lessons and Carols Service on Sunday and preside at two services on Christmas Eve. He asked if I'd preach on Christmas Day. At the thought of preaching, I got sudden stage fright or something. I didn't think I could do it.

I had preached very little since coming from California — the last three years. I did a service at Gethsemane on the fourth of July — a Wednesday night service with five people there and one pulpit supply service. I had not fully recovered from the angry pastor encounter at Incarnation. What a struggle that was for me — I confessed my part of it, I prayed to be forgiving. Several years after the event when reading a book by Nelson Mandela advocating reconciliation, I had coffee with that pastor. He had retired. I told him I kept seeing his angry face and needed to get a different view. He spent the hour telling me how difficult it was for him after I left. He had to lead all those groups and do all the pastoral care. It was all about him as it had been when I was there. That hurt continued to be unresolved and hover over me.

Now at All Saints as I read the lessons for Christmas Day and prayed, I knew I could preach and told Pastor Tim so on Sunday. He said he didn't want to pressure me. "You can just be yourself," he said. "You don't have to be me or anyone else here." I found grace flowing, support and affirmation, collegial discussion and guidance if I asked.

Christmas was over, and I was asked if I wanted to continue. And I did. The associate resigned, and I continued until a new associate was hired a year later.

For me it was a fun ministry; doing Bible Studies on the Book of Acts and with the Thursday group, leading the services and preaching at the three services in rotation, doing pastoral care. It was grace filled — and healing. Thank you, Pastor Tim.

I don't understand why it was so difficult to heal. But I praise God it happened!

If you have that problem — a hurt that is hard to heal, I just suggest you keep on praying about it. Maybe a counselor could help. (I wasn't led there.) Keep asking God for guidance.

MY BUDDHIST NEIGHBOR

I walked outside on the deck with my daughter, Jane as she was leaving. A lady who was walking on the street turned to look at us. I waved, "Hi" and she came back to talk with me. She said she was Mama, a Tibetan who lived on the next street. She admired my primroses that were blooming, saying that she also liked flowers. I offered her some primroses and she graciously accepted the offer. I dug some up and she went on her way.

Mama stopped by the next week with some marigolds she had planted from seed. She worked in the housekeeping department at Methodist Hospital. She liked to walk around the neighborhood to look at the flowers and yards. She walked by quite often and stopped to chat when I was out in the yard. She invited me to come by to see her place sometime.

I stopped by her house late one Sunday afternoon. They had just returned from a weekend visit to friends who lived near Duluth. Her husband is a highly educated Buddhist scholar. In Tibet he was a monk educated by the same teachers that taught the Dalai Lama. His life was threatened when the Chinese came in 1940's after World War II, taking over their land. He evacuated to India where he taught Buddhism in a college and they were married. Now at age 82, he spent his day in prayer.

She showed me their home. They had two children, grown, married with their own families who lived nearby. One room was designated as a prayer room with many votive candles and symbols. Here is where her husband spent much of his time. When we returned to the living room, her husband was sitting on a daybed with his legs crossed in front of him. I thought he looked like a live buddha.

Mama introduced me to him. He didn't speak English. She said, "He likes you." I said to him," We have a lot in common. You meditate. I do contemplative prayer. You are a leader in your religious group, I'm a pastor in mine. We both worship one God. I like you, too."

"Maybe you can tell me about Jesus," he said with his wife interpreting. "I'd love to tell you about Jesus," I said, "but maybe another time since I think it's time for me to go now. I've so enjoyed meeting you and you lovely wife. One thing I can tell you is that Jesus loves you."

I didn't stay that day because Mama told me they had just arrived home and were tired from the weekend. I had already been there an hour and wanted to respect Mama's needs.

I left, praising God that he wanted to hear about Jesus! I began looking for a Bible in Tibetan language. How great to have internet to search. I started with the American Bible Society — they referred me on — I found only one copy of the Tibetan Language Bible available from all the sources I found on the Internet and it cost $100! I ordered it. I also ordered seven copies of a booklet in Tibetan Language with forty-eight pages with Bible verses about the attributes of Jesus, i.e. Jesus as Savior, Jesus as Shepherd, Jesus as Redeemer etc. I also ordered copies of the same in English but when they arrived, I received Tibetan and Spanish copies. I never really got to read the booklet.

I had stopped several times before the material arrived. One time his cousin was there caring for him, bringing his dinner. He recommended I get the movie, "Seven Years in Tibet," which I watched several times. It helped me understand his loss of country and identity, his suffering and pain. In the 1990's their family along with thousands of Tibetans came to the United States. Mama estimated there were over one thousand in the Hopkins area. As I talked about my experience, I heard there were

Tibetans doing housekeeping work at Abbott Hospital. I met a young Tibetan man who was doing nursing assistance work at The Glenn Care Center. I learned that Tibetans are very open to new ideas, to learning.

After several attempts, I got to deliver the Bible and booklet to him and we could talk about Jesus. He told me when he was a teenager, several Catholic Sisters visited their village in Tibet and they were so kind. They came to help his people but soon after they came, the government forbid them, so they couldn't come anymore. They had told him about Jesus and he wanted to know more.

His first question for me was, "What do you think will happen to you when you die?"

"When I die, I'll go to heaven and be with Jesus!" I said brightly.

"What if you don't know Jesus?"

"The Bible speaks of darkness and chaos — but you can learn about Jesus now. You can come to know him. And I believe we will all see Jesus when we die and have the opportunity to confess our faith in Him."

He wanted to know how I could be so young. He was eighty-two, I was eighty-five. He was having difficulty walking. His wife said he spent much time in prayer and meditation (with little physical activity). I said I had been a health nurse, I knew I had to be active, and eat healthy. I kept busy gardening and caring for my house, exercising. Secondly, I had good genes. My parents and grandparents had lived long lives. But most importantly, I was blessed by God with good health and a clear head.

I tried to come back to talk to him about Jesus and give my witness to him. His wife said he was disturbed by the readings and couldn't talk with me.

Mama told me she was so very busy. She works five days a week. On her days off, she cares for her daughter's preschool children, so her daughter can work. Her grandson has problems; overactive, (autistic?), needing special therapy, difficult to handle. Her husband needs to be assisted with daily needs. She has relatives who assist him when she works. Mama, almost at retirement age, said she didn't have time or energy for translating and my visits. I withdrew, saying I understood.

I pray that the Holy Spirit is speaking to them about Jesus through the Living Word. I was disappointed that I couldn't do more.

I've learned that God puts me into a situation and pulls me out. I pray that I'm doing God's appointed task while I'm there. Maybe this is connected to the perception that in the personality types of earth, water, wind and fire, I am wind. I blow about, here today, gone tomorrow, it seems. I pretty much have loose connections. The Greek word for Spirit is the same as for wind. My ministry was strongly connected to Pentecost and the Holy Spirit. I was called to seminary, graduated from the seminary and received my first call on Pentecost, the day every year that we celebrate the coming of the Holy Spirit.

Have you ever found that you are done when you think you've just begun?

YOU WANT TO PRAY

I started doing Centering Prayer about 1988. Sometimes I've followed the guidelines, spending twenty minutes twice a day quiet before the Lord. More often it has been once a day or even with wide lapses in between sessions. Having a group to pray with is such a great help for me so I have started groups in several places. Here in Hopkins, a Catholic Presentation Sister, Sister Janet met with me for dinner with prayer following every week for several years until I started a group at All Saints and we joined with them. That group faded. I was back at Gethsemane and I started a group there. Linda joined us and Janet moved to Chicago.

It was Monday, the first week of February when Linda and her husband went to Florida for the month. I was thinking about that and whispered a prayer for her, wishing I had someone to pray with.

About suppertime a short time later the phone rang. A young lady on the line asked if our prayer group met on Monday night. I started to tell her we'd changed to Monday morning but then realized, "But you want to pray! Come to my house at seven and we will do Centering Prayer together." She sounded so eager.

When she came, she said she was in a rough place and this was so helpful for her. She was new to the area and needed a friendly face. She had made contact by internet. She was an answer to my prayer and I to hers. What a joy it is to have her in our prayer group and to have her as a friend.

Why do I do Centering Prayer? It's an intentional prayer. I sit and try — intend to center on God, not get into the thoughts that keep flying past in my mind. My mind flits off on thinking what I have to do later, what I'll fix for dinner, or something else. I call my focus back with my sacred word and try — intend again to open my mind, leaving a crack where God can get in and I can hear God's word for me. Centering Prayer for me has been healing, it has drawn me closer to God, it has helped me hear that guiding voice. It's like resting with Jesus. Making space for God in my life. Big decisions have been easy like when to move back to Minnesota, whether to paint the house or put on new siding, when to quit doing services in senior care centers and to begin writing this book!

We had Centering Prayer today. All four of us were here. It was uplifting to support each other, to discuss the Scriptures together, and then to pray together.

Thank you, Jesus for hearing and answering my prayers. And thank you for all the God Moments that you've given me. I know I can depend on you. Praise you!

GOD IS STILL TAKING CARE OF ME

It's about a year ago I was to pick up my friend and drive to our state capital to view the newly renovated building. I've been back in the area ten years or more but haven't driven much in these areas. That morning I prayed for special guidance and protection as I prepared to leave my home.

I found what I thought was Donna's address with my GPS and realized it wasn't the correct place. I phoned her, and she said she wasn't in Minneapolis but in Roseville with the same street address. I found the correct address and was just a few minutes late. We drove to St. Paul and the capitol area. She had researched parking but the lot she identified was full. It took extra time to find another lot and it was getting close to the time of our tour. We hopped out of the car, making our way to the Pay Box which neither of us knew how to use. With several tries, we paid for our parking space.

We arrived at the tour site about five minutes late and we could join them as they were just beginning. Minnesota State Capitol is beautiful, and it was a fun tour.

We left the building by a different door that the one we had come in. We walked to what we thought was our parking lot, but my car wasn't there. I located my parking ticket and found, sure enough, we were at the wrong lot. A passerby pointed us in the right direction and yes, there was my car. I was looking for my keys — not to be found. Arriving at the car, I found the door unlocked and the key in the ignition! I'd done it again. Left the key in the car but praise God, no one had disturbed it.

174

We had a nice visit over lunch and I took Donna back to her apartment. She had recently sold her home, moving into a senior housing apartment. She was enjoying her new living arrangement.

I stopped at Michael's to pick up a picture frame. After I checked out, a woman came up to me, handing me my gloves, saying, "These must be your gloves. They were in the shopping cart."

I guess I need lots of help and God certainly did take care of me that day! Thank you, Lord Jesus.

How many times do I not notice God's care? Or forget to say, "Thank you?"

Acknowledgments

Beattie, Melody, <u>Codependent No More: How to Stop Controlling Others and Start Caring for Yourself</u>, Hazelden, 1986.

Daly, Mary, <u>Gyn/Ecology: The Metaethics of Radical Feminism</u>, Beacon Press, 1990.

Gilligan, Carol, <u>In a Different Voice: Psychological Theory and Women's Development</u>, Harvard University Press, 1982,2016.

Nouwen, Henri, <u>The Wounded Healer: Ministry in Contemporary Society</u>, Image Books, 1979.

Poling, James Newton, <u>The Abuse of Power: A Theological Problem</u>, Abingdon Press, 1991.

Smith, Christine M., <u>Weaving the Sermon: Preaching in a Feminist Perspective</u>, Westminster John Knox Press; 1989.

Trible, Phyllis, <u>Texts of Terror: Literary-Feminist Readings of Biblical Narratives (Overtures to Biblical Theology)</u>, Fortress Press, 1984.

Hymns:
"Spirit Song", by John Wimber, Mercy Publishing, 1979.

"This is My Song", words by Lloyd Stone and Georgia Harkness, 1934: Music by Jean Sibelius, 1899.

I would like to thank all of the many people who have supported me and taught me through the years: my parents, my siblings, my children, my friends, counselors, pastors, professors and others. Special thanks to Char Torkelson and my writing group for their inspiration and guidance. I'd like to name you all, but I know my list would be incomplete. Someone recently talking to me about this book said, "I finally understand it now. It's the whole community that is involved. It's not just you." So true. So many people are involved in these stories, so many without names. But most importantly, I'd like to thank God the Father/Mother Creator, Jesus Christ, my Savior, my Friend, and the Holy Spirit for the love, the inspiration, and the direction.

Made in the USA
Middletown, DE
31 January 2019